*Dea*
*time (2 years) this little book*
*moved Eastward to you*
*In love*

# When The Sun
# Moves Northward

Cover Art by *Jane A. Evans*

# When The Sun Moves Northward

## The Way of Initiation

MABEL COLLINS

*This publication made possible with
the assistance of the Kern Foundation*

The Theosophical Publishing House
Wheaton, Ill. U.S.A.
Madras, India / London, England

© Copyright, 1987, The Theosophical Publishing House
First Quest edition, 1987. All rights reserved.

A publication of the Theosophical Publishing House, a department of the Theosophical Society in America.

Library of Congress Cataloging in Publication Data

Collins, Mabel, 1851-1927.
　　When the sun moves northward.

　　(Quest books)
　　1. Spiritual life.　I. Title.　II. Series.
BL624.C645　1987　　　299'.934　　　86-40402
ISBN 0-8356-0614-7 (pbk.)

Printed in the United States of America

No great sacrifice can commence during the Sun's southern progress. The South is Yama's quarter: Yama is the God of the Dead.

A Brahmana of the Satapatha-Brahmans says—When the sun moves northward he is among the gods, he guards the gods.

*The Buddhist Praying Wheel*

It is Time that burneth creatures, and it is Time that extinguisheth the fire.

Mahabharata

# *CONTENTS*

I am often asked about the question of time in regard to the great Ceremonies which take place at midnight when the spirits of men are most completely released from their bodies during the recurrent periods of light and darkness on the earth.

Midnight means the deepest depth of the darkness: it has no connection wit the arbitrary hours. Therefore in time there is necessarily a difference according to what places on the earth the disciples are dwelling it: and, as time does not exist except as an arbitrary temporary convenience, once outside the body man loses the sense of it.

Mabel Collins, 1923

# FOREWORD

Mabel Collins, daughter of the well-known novelist and poet Mortimer Collins and reportedly a woman of striking beauty, was a prolific writer of both fiction and nonfiction. For a time she served as assistant editor of *Lucifer*, a journal edited by Helena Blavatsky, author of *The Secret Doctrine*. She penned the theosophical classic *Light on the Path* (1885) and *The Idyll of the White Lotus* (1890), a fictionalized account of an initiation. In these, as in all her spiritual writing including the present volume, she displays a concise yet exquisitely subtle awareness of inner realities, both in the self and in the universe. Her smooth, limpid prose flows so clearly that one is carried along without effort; yet one lays down her little books feeling sure that they will never be forgotten, nor will one be spiritually the same as before.

*When the Sun Moves Northward*, first published in 1923, is such a book. This classic is taken from the apex of the mountain of the Western esoteric tradition. Founded on profound but unostentatious occult learning, it distills out the essence of several of that tradition's grand themes—astrology, initiation, man as microcosm, the idea of the master— to present their inner beauty shorn of all superfluity. Nothing of power is gone, however, and to read this book is to embark on a marvelous journey, like a high dream, through time and inward space toward imperishable treasure.

Several forceful motifs are brought together in the compass of this short work on the way of initiation. First, one does not merely read about, but feels and knows from within, the great truth of esotericism—the unity of human and cosmic cycles. This truth underlies astrology, but the ordinary use of that ancient art hardly touches its surface.

*When the Sun Moves Northward* probes deeper to correlate profoundly the progress of the solar year and the stages of human inward initiation.

Second, this book displays the visionary sweep that counterbalances esotericism's often sane but stodgy rationalism. Here in one evocative scene after another, color, scent, and mood combine to make almost visible and tangible the chapels and initiatory halls that represent the stages of the great quest. Whether they are subjective or objective places the seeress never discloses; one learns the salutary lesson that it does not matter, so long as the pilgrim of the sun comes at last to Easter dawn.

Third, Collins's work shows brilliantly that the real heart of esotericism, as of the true Christian mysticism with which she freely correlates it, is neither psychism nor arcane knowledge, but great spiritual realities: joy, death and rebirth, and above all love. One could wish that love was given such a central place by all occultists.

Finally, the volume provides interesting information on the esoteric background of the earlier classic *Light on the Path.*

The reader turning the pages of this little book will live through an adventure from which, like the sun on its northward pilgrimage through the months, he will return, but he will not return to the same place in his spiritual journey. He will have moved on, perhaps only slightly, perhaps a great distance.

ROBERT ELLWOOD
Bashford Professor of
Oriental Studies, University
of Southern California

# DECEMBER
## *The Birth Month*


Ceremonies and Feasts

1st. The Ceremony of Desire of Birth

5th. The Ceremony of Terror

7th. The Ceremony of Consecration

11th. The Feast of Love

15th. The Feast of Union

21st. The Feast of Satisfaction

25th. The Birth Day

# CHAPTER I

The profound fundamental connection between the ceremonies of the great world religions and the facts of Nature is shown by the manner in which they are grouped round the story of the year. On the material plane this story begins with the universally observed festival of the New Year, which is understood to celebrate the victory of light over darkness, and culminates at the beginning of June, when the Tibetans observe the anniversary of Buddha's Nirvana. The New Year Festival is preceded by the Feasts and Ceremonies of Birth, marking the season in which the sun—the light and life of the world—enters upon rebirth, and returns to conquer darkness and death. He

comes back each year as a little child, wax-
ing strong as the seasons advance. Macrobe
says that the ancient Egyptians represented
the sun, "au solstice d'hiver sous l'image d'un
petit enfant." The student of occultism is
aware that man is a part of Nature, and that
the mysteries are revealed to him when he
enters into the secret and sacred life of the
heavens and the earth. For him the yearly
season of material birth is preceded by the
spiritual state of desire of birth. Both in the
Egyptian and Buddhist systems the sun is sup-
posed to die, or lose his fertilizing energy, in
the autumn and early winter, and Simpson,
in *The Buddhist Praying Wheel*, points out
how unlikely it is that this idea can have orig-
inated in India. He considers that the Aryans
must have brought it there from cold lati-
tudes. The difference of climate in the various parts of the earth does not affect the
religions of the world in their universal acceptance of the month of January as the
season of the return of the light of the world.
All Nature begins life anew; and the month
of December is devoted to the preparation for

this fresh life. In an article in the *Revue Egyptologique* in January, 1880, Brugsch Bey, basing his statement on an inscription, speaks of a Ceremony performed at Memphis by the Pharaoh himself, or one of the High Priests, on a certain day which owed its sanctity to the rite—the winter solstice, or 22nd December. He quotes Macrobe in respect to the sun being depicted at that period of the year as a little child. Man's spiritual being is indissolubly associated with this little child, this lightbringer, and as the disciple attains psychic consciousness he becomes aware of the mystic recurrence of that miracle which is described in the religions as birth, death, and resurrection. As he passes up the steps of consciousness, he learns that the spiritual lightbearer must endure the martyrdom of crucifixion in time and space, and must descend into the tomb of matter. And as the Great Ones in their bright succession endure this, so must their followers. The yearly initiations begin with that desire of rebirth into matter which brings the human spirit into the condition of suffering under the rule of the pairs of opposites; heat and cold, pleasure and pain, love and hate, male and female— these opposing conditions assail him continually, and he cannot free himself from them save by escaping from rebirth. It was the work of the Christ to show the meaning of the Cross, and to teach the great lesson of sacrifice which means that none shall seek Freedom till all are saved. He promised to remain with us always, renouncing His Nirvana until the end of the world, and dwelling with His beloved children—the publican and the sinner—in the mysterious inner places of consciousness. And those who follow Him must do likewise, and must enter into the state of the desire of birth each year with a yearly increase of the will to help the world. Thus the desire changes its character by degrees, and becomes selfless instead of selfish. The soul of man, and the soul of the world, the soul of Nature and of sub-Nature, all pass alike through the birth-throes.

In December, the birth month, there are seven great and vital Ceremonies, filling the whole month with their observances. The first is the Desire of Birth, the commencement of the mystic story. It is so remote from human and material life that it is impossible to describe it in human language. It is witnessed consciously only by the spiritual being before its descent into matter. The disciple who seeks to take part in it while living in the body must endeavor to recall to his psychic memory the litany which he heard chanted in the spiritual sphere from which he came when he sought the experience of human life. The Ceremony of the Desire of Birth lasts for four days and nights, beginning on 1st December. During this time it is necessary for the disciple to contemplate all that is implied in its litany. At each midnight, and at the hour of dawn, he should meditate upon the words of the litany, endeavoring to obtain understanding in respect to them. They are very difficult and obscure, so much so as to seem meaningless to the man in material life if he tests them by the light of intellect. But the disciple who belongs to one of the occult schools,[1] and who desires to become a conscious part of the Divine whole, must enter into the psychic life of the world at this sacred season, and apprehend from year to year more and more of the mystery of the divine life in himself, and its union with the material.

## THE LITANY

*I. I desire birth.*

*II. I am ready to be burned and consumed; for that is what birth is.*

*III. I am ready to be naked and unprotected, and to suffer from my nakedness; for that is what life is.*

*IV. I am ready to make the pilgrimage through matter in darkness and in fire, so that the circle of the uncreate shall become one with the circle of the create.*

The ordeal of fire which comes upon the soul immediately that the desire for birth is

---

[1]The occult schools referred to here are psychic, not physical, and the disciple is one who has entered upon the yoga of *Light on the Path.*

experienced, and continues while man remains man only, is the burning out and consuming of all alloy in the nature. When this is accomplished, the ego can effect the miracle of resurrection and rebirth into a higher state, and can begin to form a regenerated shape which shall be worthy of immortality.

The instinct of the animal nature is to avoid suffering and to seek protection from it. But the Spirit of Man has sought birth in matter with the object of obtaining purification, and desires, therefore, not only to enter the ordeal of fire but to enter it unprotected. Therefore does it utter these two stanzas of the litany which follow the expression of desire of birth. The mystic union is expressed in the last stanza; it is beyond the understanding of man. He can only dimly apprehend it by degrees as he follows the occult ceremonies, and obtains more and more illumination in respect to them. Autumn, winter, spring, and summer repeat themselves duly every year, because the Divine Spirit of Nature descends continually upon Nature, and passing through matter returns to itself. The drama is enacted afresh every year. The story of the pilgrimage of the spirit of man is contained within this yearly drama, and is the basis of the legends which form the groundwork of the great religions.

Desire, marriage, birth, these bring us hither: love, death, resurrection, these carry us hence; just as the green leaves come with every springtide, so does the inner meaning of the green leaves reveal itself to the disciple in perpetual recurrence.

The ancient Egyptians were the first to institute a sacred calendar, in which every day had its special religious ceremony. The Egyptian initiate, who gave fragments of the Birthday Litany and the Resurrection Litany from the ancient Ritual to the author of the *Story of the Year*, has now outlined the rites and vigils of the months between Christmas and Easter. But he has given nothing for the summer and autumn months, during which no existing religion has dates for ceremonies or feasts. Doubtless this is in accordance with the accepted belief of the ancients, that no great sacrifice can commence during the sun's southern progress. The south belongs to Yama, the God of the Dead. The sacred months are those in which the sun moves northwards.

# *CHAPTER II*

*I*n the first conscious experiences of the disciple, the desire of birth is followed by the sense of nothingness; in other words, the desires of power, of effort, of accomplishment, used to so great an end, leave the spirit shivering and terror-stricken; overpowered by the conviction that nothing exists, that effort is in vain and power useless, because accomplishment is impossible. In this first Ceremony, the disciple, who becomes aware that his spirit has desired birth, and recognizes his own free will, has taken the first step into new life, unfamiliar and untried conditions. It is natural that the next sensation should be that of confusion. At the entrance of the occult life this condition must be experienced.

The first time the disciple is consciously aware of it the suffering is terrible, because it seems to be a final state. It is known as the Ceremony of Terror, and two stanzas of the birth litany belong to it.

## LITANY

I. *I am nothing, save as a fragment to be burned and consumed.*
II. *I, alone, am as nothing.*

This is the season of the "Dweller on the Threshold." Before the disciple has obtained the power to enter the Hall of Learning, and witness the Ceremonies as they take place here, he becomes aware of the state of terror in the experiences of life. The indifference of the world overwhelms him like a paralyzing frost. The successful and happy pay so so little heed to misery and despair that the sufferers each seem to be alone, and the disciple, who looks round with awakening consciousness, perceives this, both for himself and for others. To the man who remains only a student of life, this terrible experience teaches philosophy, and his spirit bows before it, as in Nature he bows before the wind or succumbs to the bitter frost. The disciple who enters upon initiation, and follows the Ceremonies in their course, recognizes its recurrence with every year of growth. It attacks him upon one plane of consciousness after another, and with each upward step the ordeal becomes more awful. At last he reaches a point at which he experiences the Ceremony in its fulness, and he finds himself utterly and absolutely alone; unconscious of his higher self, of his Guide, of his Master, of his God. Then he knows he is nothing, save as a fragment to be burned and consumed. Then he knows that alone he is nothing. Then he knows he must endure the initiation and attain to union, to the companionship of the pilgrimage. The spirit within him stretches out towards others, towards its fellow sufferers in the crucifixion of human life, and this brings him into the Hall of Learning to witness the Ceremony of Consecration, and listen to the chant of the initiates.

## LITANY

I. *I devote the spirit that is being born within me to the service of the spirit of love.*

II. *In this coming year I will dwell in the sanctuary of love; I will not offend against the law of love.*

III. *I will remember that I have not to ask love but to give love; that I have to give of my very self to the world.*

IV. *I will molest none; I will forgive all. In return, I demand that the spirit to be born in me this month shall be beloved of the brotherhood of souls, and shall be recognized as a soul of love.*

While listening to this litany, the spirit of the disciple intuitively makes the profound obeisance. It has turned itself towards the light of the spiritual world—the spirit of love.

Having passed through the blackness of desolation, and learned that no possession is permanent and that no thing endures, the disciple is now prepared to offer up all that he has in the service of the divine life, which alone is eternal. He knows now that he himself is but a changing and impermanent creature, and he is ready to surrender all things in order to nourish the germ of divinity which lies hidden within himself, and so escape from the law of impermanence which governs human life.

During the Ceremony of Terror the Hall of Learning is dark and deserted, quite empty save for a dreadful sense of desolation, the doors flung wide open, and the bitter wind, that is like cruelty itself, rushes through them so that none can stand before it. At the Ceremony of Consecration the doors are closed, there is a deep sense of longing and aspiration, and the disciple becomes dimly aware of other presences around him. Silence reigns till this consciousness comes; then the faint chanting of the litany is heard, and he knows that close about him it is being inaudibly repeated by the unseen brethren of his spirit. Darkness reigns; and in the darkness the spirit kneels in its own innermost sanctuary within the heart of the ego. This is what is known in occultism as the profound obeisance. In the silence that follows the litany a voice speaks, the voice that is of the silence; the disciple can never again be alone or afraid, once having heard this. He is born anew, individualized on a higher plane, and is there recognized. Even in the midst of the ordeal of the Ceremony of Terror, he holds fast to the knowledge that it will pass, and he will find himself once again standing firmly amidst that which is real and unchanging and eternal. And then, by this obeisance of the spirit and the effort of consecration, he brings himself among the crowd of unseeing spirits which desire to become a part of the great body of love, and to devote themselves to its service. They appear on this great occasion in the ritual of initiation as a vast veiled assemblage. These are they with undeveloped capacities, who trust blindly in a God of whom they have been taught by creeds and in churches.

By intensity and purity of desire these are enabled to experience the joy and pain of absolute consecration; but they experience it in darkness—the darkness of a soul as yet unlit.

This stanza of the litany is the one most

easily understood by those who, with bandaged eyes, first hear the mystic chant, and is the one which they themselves first repeat, joining in the chant of the invisible. "I will molest none; I will forgive all. In return, I demand that the spirit to be born within me shall be beloved of the brotherhood of souls, and shall be recognized as a soul of love."

When once these great resolves are made, of molesting none, of forgiving all, the Ceremony of Consecration has been understood and fully experienced; and a degree of knowledge and of advancement is obtained which can never be lost. It is very difficult to enter at that Ceremony, more difficult still to pass through it. Most often the right and power to enter are won by conquering a feeling of justifiable resentment, of resentment against actual wrong. The surrender must be a profound one, made in the sanctuary of the spirit, and must be absolute, covering not merely a single instance of injustice or wrongdoing, but all instances of injustice or wrongdoing. Then arise in the heart the first words of the great song of life, which belong to the Feast of Love, the Feast of the Soul.

## LITANY

*I. Love is the only King;*
*The only Ruler*
*The only Creator.*

When his spirit is aware of this wondrous litany, and is able to join in the triumphant song, the Hall of Learning becomes visible to the disciple as all alive and glowing, full of an intensity of color, purple, and green. The great river that runs through it from end to end, and which is often hidden from sight, is now uncovered. It looks like a country stream in which long grasses grow in the summertime in cool lands. Reeds and rushes stand high among the grass-like groups of slender spirit shapes. The walls are all alight with jewels, which resolve themselves into words for those who are able to read. The words of the litany flame out upon them from time to time.

## LITANY

II. *Hate and Satan one; rebel, anarchist, destroyer.*

III. *Love's action is what men call charity.*

IV. *The action of hatred is known as malice.*

V. *Love has only one punishment for the sinner, and that is forgiveness.*

VI. *To live according to the law of love is a hundred thousand times harder than to live according to the law of hatred; to this great effort I pledge myself. To live according to the law of love means the acceptance of every evil as a good. By that acceptance, if it is done in the spirit of love, the evil becomes good. It is to the conversion of evil into good in our natures, in the natures of others, and in the affairs of life, that we devote ourselves. Henceforth we do not avoid evil, we love it and transform it. By loving it we make ourselves a part of the creative principle which is love.*

VII. *To this great effort the disciples pledge*

*themselves during the Feast of Love,
and bind themselves together to unite
in it. It cannot be done alone.*

Therefore it is that close upon the Feast of
Love follows the Feast of Union.

The evil which is treated of in this litany
is not sin; it is not reduced to thoughts or
words or actions. It is that force which causes
these things, and which opposes goodness as
hate opposes love, and pleasure opposes pain.
This last pair of opposites is that most easily
understood by men, and it is an early exercise of the disciple not to shrink from pain,
but to so blend it with pleasure that a new
emotion is created. The word which most
nearly expresses this new emotion in human
language is ecstasy. Love, the greatest power
known to us, obliterates hatred by its very
presence. Men continue to be cruel and bitter and revengeful, because the Brotherhood
of Love is not yet strong enough in the human
race to become dominant. Hatred yields itself
up to its opposite when love is made manifest,
because its aims and efforts are futile; it can-

not hurt or injure that spirit which is above
pain or loss, therefore it becomes inactive,
and the force which causes this passion
changes its nature. So with good and evil; by
using the supreme power of love, the force
which rushes in upon men's souls, causing
outbursts of crime and cruelty, can be stayed
in its course, and so overpowered by the love
spirit that its nature is changed. It is necessary
to remember that men are swayed and influ-
enced by forces which sweep over the
thought-world as winds sweep over the earth,
or as currents of electricity flash through the
ether. Practical scientists aim at controlling
the forces of Nature, alchemists aim at changing the character of material substances. The
practical occultist aims at controlling the
forces of human nature and changing the
character of thought-substance; that is the
profession to which he is devoted; not his own
development, nor the influencing of individ-
uals, form his chief work. As he develops, he
finds himself encountering the powers and
forces which assail him in common with the
rest of the race; strong in his position as a soul

of love, he is unhurt by hatred or evil, and can unite with others, equally well equipped, to influence the thought-substance of the world. When the pairs of opposites are blended, under the dominion of the love spirit, a great wave of new life and strength breaks in upon men, because the struggle has ceased, and instead of men's souls being torn in opposite directions, they are uplifted towards the infinite Good by a greatly increased impulse. It is as though two hands, which had been plucking man's soul into two parts, were suddenly placed together and used to uplift him. This effect cannot continue, while man is under the law of the pairs of opposites, crucified, unless the effort which caused it is continuous. Conditions immediately relapse into their normal state of friction and struggle when the effort is relaxed. None can essay this effort but those who are purified by the spiritual fire, firm in the body of spiritual love, secured in the consciousness of the Supreme. It is because few are fitted for this work that the race remains a prey to conflict and sin and cruelty.

The disciple has desired to be born; and has passed successfully through the ordeal of fire. He has chanted the litany: "I am ready to be burned and consumed; for that is what birth is." He has suffered at the hands of the "seven great officiating priests." All experience has been tested and consumed in the blaze of the Vaisvana fire *(Bhagavad Gita)*. He is naked and unprotected, stripped of all delusion; a spirit purified, standing out of the fire of purification. He is pledged now to live according to the law of love; the hardest life possible for the embodied spirit of man, for it means the entrance into the little army capable of accepting and transmuting evil. To fight this force is the task of the novice, in his own nature; he encounters it continually upon the battlefield of his being, from incarnation to incarnation. Being now self-restrained and enlightened, the disciple is able, in union with other disciples equally purified, to stand before the great and terrible force of evil, and lessen its baleful influence upon the race by influencing and changing its character. He enters, being now a part of the creative spirit of love, upon the task of the alchemist who transmutes and changes. In the strengthening of this band of workers, in whom the Christos is developed, lies the hope of emancipation of the race. Mankind, as a whole, is too deeply submerged in matter, and too much under the influence of material thought, to be capable of development while the evil force is so powerful. It is for the leaders, the disciples, and the initiates who guide them from beyond the gateway of material life, to give to the race its great hope and opportunity. The disciple who has triumphed over the first pair of opposites (pleasure and pain) in his own nature, who has passed over the steps of human life in successive incarnations, and been utterly burned in the sacrificial fire, can henceforth stand without fear before the evil force. It cannot injure him. But he cannot change or alter its character, alone; therefore does the Feast of Union follow the Feast of Love.

When he is bidden to enter on this task, he finds himself in his own place, from which he cannot be cast down, save by his own fault. And so severely has he been tested that fault in him is not looked for. But because fault or failure is always possible, each takes the vow not to swerve or falter though the one next him should be cast down or removed far from him. He becomes aware then of the great and awful Thing which is Evil; a Power so dreadful that man, as man, can only fight it in blind unseeing warfare, as it attacks him in different parts of his nature, physical and psychic. Were he to see and know what mighty thing this is that sweeps over his soul, he would succumb utterly; because he has not yet entered into the infinitely mighty power of Love. Blood-red is the color of Evil, and when the disciples encounter the force, it lies with them to wash away its stain and replace it with pure whiteness. Absolute selflessness creates a crystalline quality which effaces the fierce red of the evil power. It obliterates the vivid coloring of flowers and jewels, as though their brilliance were blotted out by a greater glory; as intense sunlight produces an impression of colorless brightness.

In the splendor of the Love Feast all things in the place of learning, even when others see blood red and fire color, have the whiteness of the white lily to the selfless one. It is only possible to be aware of this whiteness when the heart has opened itself, not only to those who give joy and pleasure, but also to the great, sad outside world which but to think of causes pain and weariness. No one who has ever seen this whiteness can rest again in the sloth of indifference. It is seen only in the intensity of the Love Feast, when the man gives out from himself to the whole world without reservation or possibility of withdrawal. At the Feast of Union, which follows immediately, the Hall looks glorious with color. To those who have successfully passed through the ordeals of consecration and sacrifice, the whiteness, seen for a long awe-inspiring moment, yields to clouds of glorious color. Flaming jewels flash on the walls, amethyst and sapphire; a carpet of growing pansies and violets appears upon the ground. And all the shapes of men, standing close together in that mystic space, breathe the litany together in a mere whisper, yet in perfect unison.

## LITANY

   I. *There is no more any parting of the ways.*

  II. *All the different paths are become but the one path.*

 III. *I am but a part.*

 IV. *I am but one stone in the Great Temple.*

  V. *I am a soldier in the army, and from the one who is next me I cannot swerve by ever so small a fraction; for if I did, the march of the whole army would be disordered. I remain, therefore, immovably associated with my fellow soldiers.*

 VI. *I know that I take upon myself the responsibility of the whole when I pass consciously into union with it.*

VII. *I am ready, without complaint, to be cast down from the place in which I stand, should I swerve or flinch under any trial falling on those next me; for*

*I know that my strength can never be exhausted, since my comrades also stand unswervingly by my side; and while united we cannot fall.*

It must be remembered that the expressions used in these litanies are mystical. The nearness spoken of, the comradeship and union, are entirely spiritual, and have no reference to any nearness or association on the physical plane. There is, indeed, a psychic nearness which does not come within the meaning of these esoteric expressions. The disciple, who has become a recognized unit in the great army, has entered upon that place where there are footprints solid as though cut in rock, because through the ages, and before Time was, each one who has entered upon the great path has of necessity stepped in the prints of the feet of the one who has gone before him. The steps of all are identical. *The one who walks* is the Sovereign Lord, the human Ego, who moves consciously on through birth and rebirth. And only this higher self of man, in its full consciousness, can realize the intense reality and solidity of spiritual life; how brilliant the light of the spiritual sun, how firm that which is beneath the footsteps of the one who can walk. The unreality and impermanence of physical and material life are as things in a passing dream to the one who has entered into the state of union. Love alone can bring him to that state. Hatred is an emotion peculiar to the physical spheres, a direct outcome of their special constitution. He who desires to escape from physical life can only do so by passing into and through the School of Love; there is no other way. Therefore all those who enter selfishly upon the path of occultism, and essay the practices belonging to it, while still animated by personal motives, become evil powers, children of the darkness, and find themselves eventually more grossly and absolutely material than the materialists themselves. The occultist's whole being and nature is as a garden highly tended, instead of a piece of arid land; and if a weed grows in that rich soil, it becomes a giant, and cannot be uprooted for long ages.

The army of Love moves as one man because there can be no misunderstanding and no mistake. The union is absolute, and nothing less is of any avail. How many steps and experiences must be passed before it can be attained! What is called love in ordinary human language is the first step, a perpetual invitation placed before us, urging us to the stupendous essay. When the state of occult union is reached, it may be that the one nearest, from whom it is not permitted to swerve, is dwelling afar. It is possible that soldiers in this mystic army have never been embodied at the same time, and have never exchanged human speech, although through ages they have stood side by side. The human being whose nearest and dearest is in a high spiritual place, and whose conduct and actions are ruled by the same law as that which governs his comrade (which is the meaning of neither swerving nor wavering), is one of those who are lights to their neighbors and associates on the physical plane.

Those who are incapable of using Love as a first step, and passing to the next, pressing on till they can pass this ceremony consciously, must fall back again and again, no matter how strong their aspirations or how great their gifts. For he who stands alone, stands but to fall.

Love is a miraculous thing. It resembles only that which is miraculous in life, and can be compared only to that. Its birth in the soul is marvelous and inexplicable, as is the birth of the soul in the body. Once it is born it grows steadily till it has the capacity to appreciate all that lives, to suffer with all that lives, to be responsible for all that lives. And so, no matter what changes take place around the disciple in external life, within himself he is bound to remain immovable, knowing that the real union is unchanged, and but grows the more intense for apparent severance. Even though the one next you (in ordinary language, your soul comrade, the one among the innumerable hosts whom you love best) be removed externally, to a distant place, to another planet, or to the footstool of God's throne, yet you may not swerve or flinch, but must retain unimpaired the sense of union. The mystic sense which binds spirits in indissoluble bonds must be capable of conquering distance, so that the very universe can be spanned, if need be; it holds together master and pupil, adept and disciple, man and angel. From it arises the state known as the "Feast of Satisfaction," a condition of uttermost content, the self being absorbed in the whole. A disciple who consciously witnessed the celebration of this feast in the Hall of Learning wrote down the following description, which, brief as it is, contains some vital details:

"In my effort to reach the Hall, I seemed at first to lose my way. I found myself in a high thicket of myrtle, which was all in flower. Above me was the blue sky. For a moment I was full of a keen consciousness of the sweet fresh air and sunshine, and the strength and joy of the plants. Then, as I looked, the myrtle was all gathered and thrown upon the ground, covering the great floor of the Hall. Someone who stood beside me said, 'Behold, the harvest has been laid low. The little tree of personal life has been cut down; it lies beneath the feet of the *one who walks,* and with every step it gives forth an inexpressibly sweet fragrance, which will never again depart from him.' "

This fragrance is that mysterious product of the incarnations which remains with the ego thenceforth, when incarnations are at an end. But it comes only from the trampled myrtle; the personal self must be cut down, and cast down, and walked upon, before that fragrance arises.

## LITANY

    I. *The divine satisfaction has fallen upon me.*

   II. *I give because my heart is too full; it cannot contain all that it has.*

  III. *I am conscious that love is infinite, though I can hold but one drop. Therefore do I cut down the little tree which was the expression of my personal growth.*

  IV. *Here, on the floor of the place of learning, lies the myrtle of my life; then it will wither, and it will be*

*swept away when the floor is prepared
for the next great Feast. I am satisfied
that this is so, for I have entered into
all.*

   V. *I myself am nothing and have
nothing.*

  VI. *Yet I have all and I am all.*

 VII. *I sleep and wake at the same time.*

VIII. *Within me is the measureless content
which is eternal rest, and which, once
attained, can never be disturbed. My
being is absorbed with the absolute
peace, therefore I am ready for ceaseless activity, and armed for incessant
warfare.*

Immortality and Love are almost identical; they cannot be separated.

Oh, sleeping souls that go blindly on to
death, be warned, and awake! There is no
death for those that live love. See, then, that
you open your hearts and let the green leaves
of spring burst forth within them, making
new life for those who look upon the miracle
taking place within you. Those to whom your

tenderness is given will taste the sweetness of divine life, will witness the majesty of resurrection, will themselves become aware of the power of the unseen.

When the "one who walks" looks down upon the scattered and withering myrtles, amongst which lies the little tree of his own personal life, he is prepared to encounter all misfortune or hardship, because he realizes for how short a time it can last. Only that which affects his immortal being is of any permanent importance. This the disciple has known intellectually since first his mind awakened; but now that he is entering into the consciousness of the whole, he for the first time perceives it actually. That which was himself but a little while ago lies there now a withered branch. Yet the higher self has all and is all.

The sign of the neophyte or newly planted one, the triangle, typifies the condition of sleeping and waking at the same time, and the mystic state of ecstasy which arises from this condition. Later on the cross comes within it, that new cross of the higher suffering;

the suffering in and with all humanity, the cross on which the Christos of man is continually crucified, as well as the Christ Himself.

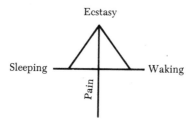

# CHAPTER III

The Feast of Birth is the second great feast of the year, the first in dignity being that of Easter. It is the second in importance, and in difficulty; consequently there are fewer present at it than at any of the preliminary Ceremonies, for the simple reason that few are able to endure it. Many who have passed through the others, and have hoped by the experience gained in them to find strength for the greater ordeal, have failed and faltered at the entrance to the Hall of Learning. Some who enter turn back at the sight of the great river which, in its silence and stillness, effects the ordeal. For at the hour of birth, at the supreme moment, the soul gazes upon itself in these waters. Few have the strength to do this. Those who have endured this ordeal then join in the utterance of the single stanza which forms the litany of the birthday.

## LITANY

*I desire absolute Love.*

The spirit about to be born into a new world asks of that world Love. He puts out helpless hands towards those who are already born. The appeal of the infant child is that which forms the universal litany of the birthday of Christ and the Christ man.

The birth color is pale pink, and the Hall is seen during this Feast, by disciples and initiates alike, as of the color of wild roses. The atmosphere seems to be full of light clouds, and these clouds might be great bunches of roses without leaves. Here and there, where the color is warmer, out of the heart of the deeper tint there arises from time to time a vivid fork of flame; this is caused by the flash of thought and feeling which is the birth of a soul.

The great river is open and clear, and it is like an immense mirror. The disciples, as they enter, pass down to its margin and gaze intently into its depths for a while, then give place to others. Many shrink back at the last moment, for in the still water a formidable vision is seen, a strange and terrible picture arises and forms itself for each one. The disciple who can endure this initiation sees his own life, his past history, shown as in a looking-glass, without any blurring or softening or any hiding away. The facts are there in their simplicity, without excuse or disguise. Some stories told by the water, some pictures shown, are very beautiful; for human life is full of beauty. The man will stand amazed sometimes at the unexpected loveliness of a past deed. Other pictures stand out in shameful clearness, some sordid, some terrible. The disciple who is strong enough to endure it remains gazing in fascination upon this inexorable record, this resolute recapitulation, which does not cease till all is seen, and all is told, and all the sum of the life is added up and reckoned accurately. Having watched the changing pictures in the mirror of water till all told and done, the disciple passes on, giving place to others, and enters the mysterious place known as the Chapel of Fire, where that warm color that comes out of the rose-tinted clouds becomes concentrated and makes a great flame. Into this the disciple enters. It is like passing into the fierceness of a great furnace. He finds himself impelled to enter in, unveiled, unprotected, all sheaths and vestures (even the animal soul itself) having fallen away. He who can endure this will look upon himself and know himself, when the flame of birth rises out of the rose color. The initiates who watch the Ceremonies know, when the flame of birth springs forth, that a disciple has endured throughout the initiation, has chosen birth, and is born.

The one who is born passes out of the rose color into a place of dusky silence. The whole of the birth ceremonies and feasts being accomplished, a period of vigils, of fasting, of prayer, sets in. The new-born one has to bear the cross of the higher life. Emotion and desire have carried him thus far, endurance and growth must prepare him for the experiences of the sacred months which follow that devoted to birth. Before him now lie the mystic vigils and feasts in which death, resurrection, and transmutation are symbolized and shown.

The actual birthday is reached. Now comes the opening of the golden gate, the lifting of the heavy iron bar that clasps and holds it.

# JANUARY
## The Love Vigil

# NEW YEAR'S DAY

### Words from the Master in Love
### to the Disciple

#### I

Brave heart it is that sees the light!
　　Strong soul that scents the fragrant air.
None else can hope to scale the height:
　　None else can breathe the silent prayer.

#### II

Put Pleasure back and let her laugh,
　　Bid peace turn her pale face from thee;
In them you find a changeling half
　　Of that great joy that lives in me.

#### III

I bid my children look afar
　　To where I stand alone and wait.
Push back the heavy iron bar
　　That clasps and holds the golden gate.

#### IV

Yes, push it back; for in your hands
　　My strength lies waiting for your will.
Enter with me the shining lands,
　　Climb thou with me the golden hill.

#### V

But know that slaves have there no place.
　　Pleasure or pride, or peace or pain,
These bring no changes on thy face;
　　As my power waxes theirs must wane.

*Green Leaves*

# CHAPTER IV
### *What light is to Nature, love is to the heart of man*

*T*he Master in love speaks to the disciples on the first day of the new year, for in the first month of the year the love vigils are held, those vigils in which the disciple is prepared and made strong for all the experiences which follow, and which try and test him to the uttermost. The gates have been firmly closed, the iron bar is heavy to lift, the disciple cannot lift it alone.

The gates of gold are those portals which admit to the spiritual life. They do not *close* on it—they admit to it. It is the iron bar that lies across them which alone prevents their standing always ajar, ready to yield softly to the touch of any who would enter. But the iron bar is very heavy and hard to push aside —so heavy that none can do it alone. The iron bar, so heavy, so firm, so inexorable, is an illusion; it is that artificial and temporary consciousness which makes of men separate and isolated beings. To the man who regards things from the external standpoint, this consciousness appears to be the one great reality, the one absolute truth, so profound is the state of illusion in which he dwells.

The new year, the season of the return of light and heat, and of the renewed upspringing of the fertilizing life, brings the idea of hope to men. Though the gates are closed and the iron bar is heavy to lift, that is only for the moment. The change will come, the miracle will take place, the resurrection is sure. Remember there are always the buds in spring; the green leaves of the heart will burst forth in due time. And remember that super-Nature is certain and inexorable as is Nature; and the eternal laws of the greater can be learned by studying those of the lesser.

As the sun returns again, bringing beauty

to the natural world, so the divine light
returns again, bringing love, the most beautiful of all things. The heart becomes barren
by torture. Disappointment, grief, regret, re-
morse, and shame strip the green leaves from
it, and fling them to wither on the ground.
They are the bitter winds and cruel frosts of
man's nature. Youth and joy are gone it seems
forever. Faith, which is unconscious knowledge, is necessary to the disciple who would
take part in this miracle. The "Words of the
Master in Love to the Disciple" are addressed
to those who have reached this point, who
may perhaps fall back from the golden gates,
fainting on the very threshold, because their
knowledge has not yet become perfected.

If the obedient one has patience, and wills
to endure, he will find himself suddenly
clothed again with brightness, and aware of
the divine warmth. It is faith which enables
this miracle to take place; faith, not in a creed
or an altar, but in the unseen life and its laws
of recurrence. Faith and confidence are qualities which are essential to the disciple.

The whole of January, this month of be-

ginning, is devoted to the ceremonial of the
School of Love, and every dawn, every noon,
every midnight in the month has its prayer
to be uttered in unison. These prayers can be
made known only to those who have actually entered the school. To other disciples the
doctrine of the school is imparted by one of
its masters, at this season; and all who are
endeavoring to enter the high path in earnest
can take part in this month-long vigil. The
deep violet-blue, which is the love color, per-
vades the Hall of Learning throughout the
vigil, and the disciple may know by his per-
ception of this whether he is obtaining entrance to the school, and what degree of
advancement in it he has reached. The observance of the vigil gives strength to the disciple for the endurance of the later feasts of the
mystic months; and therefore it is well to
enter into the place of learning continually,
all through it, for strength is given forth, as
from a fountain, when the masters in love
assemble. At the Resurrection Festival only
those who are accepted members of the
school are able to enter within the doors.

The disciple who would enter the School of Love must pass through a severe preparation, and must have attained possession of the five qualities and seven attributes which mark these scholars. The two first qualities are Faith and Confidence; the third is the Gift of Charity, which makes the forgiveness of offenses a natural act, not an enforced one. When the disciple can attain to this, he renders up all the weapons of offense or warfare. No longer does he wish that he shall have peace or power or pleasure, for himself or for any loved one. All motive for combat with any other, or even for defense from any other, is gone, once and for all. Then the spirit of the disciple becomes as a dove that is clothed in white plumage. If in his person power be seen, or if by him force is used, that power and force come from the great brotherhood of love, not from himself, and are guided by its masters. Power and force can be equally instruments of evil or of good; and men frequently work evil by exercising them, even when acting with the highest motives. Nor can the disciple trust himself to use them, unless he is a scholar in this sublime school, and knows that those wiser than himself are acting upon and through him. Therefore, the disciple can be a student only, not an active agent in the world of men, before his entrance into this school. He must suffer the preparation, and examine himself constantly to ascertain whether he has attained the required qualities and attributes. The qualities are—

*First*, the Capacity for Faith, or Unconscious Knowledge.

*Second*, the Divine Confidence, or Hope Inextinguishable.

*Third*, The Gift of Charity.

*Fourth*, The Power of Pure Love, which gives without expectation of any return.

*Fifth*, the Consciousness of the Unseen, or the Knowledge of super-Nature.

The attributes are partly psychic and partly intellectual. Discernment, reason, justice, honor, are recognizable by the human mind, and are therefore called intellectual. The vision of the inner eye, the hearing of the inner ear, the sense of spiritual touch are purely psychic, and their use, to the disciple, is that of spiritual enlightenment. There are many more psychic attributes which develop as the whole psychic man comes to his full growth; but these seven are necessary to the disciple before he can learn the first lesson in the School of Love, or pass the first initiation.

He who enters the body of love must yield up all, even his own soul, at the entrance. Before he can be recognized by the brethren in love, he must take his animal self and lay it beneath his feet, planting his foot upon its neck. Before he can become aware of the existence of the masters in love, he must kill out that blinding folly which makes men hunger for separate life. Before any welcome can be uttered to him, he must seize the very nature that quivers within him, and which causes him to live, and compel it to be silent and still. Otherwise it would drown out that welcome, should it be uttered, by its outcry for mercy. Have no pity for it, or it will become your ruler.

It is the emotions only which admit to the

citadel of the soul; it is through the heart only
that you can reach yourself. It is through love
you must learn. Dwell upon this miraculous
thing, cultivate it, study it. Take your heart
and all its emotions, divest them of all covering and gaze upon them. Learn to do so crit-
ically and without flinching. Deal thus not
only with your own heart, but also with the
hearts of your true companions. Only from
those who are true can truth be obtained.
Suffer cheerfully, knowing that by suffering
your grossest parts of self are burned out and
consumed. In the experience of the heart, and
in the lessons of love, there are both profound
pleasure and acute torture. If you lend yourself glady to the torture, the sooner will it be
ended. Gaze on your heart unflinchingly and
learn of it. Do not fear the hard names your
animal soul will use towards your great self.
Defy those lower instincts which drag you
back towards unconsciousness. The disciple
who makes the demand to enter upon this
vigil must remember that this means an invitation to suffering, which suffering surely
will speedily fall upon him with a severity

that to an ordinary man would be insupportable.

The demand for psychic consciousness has to be repeated many times before the vision of the inner eyes, the hearing of the inner ears, the sense of spiritual touch, are obtained. Many disciples seek these year after year, entering the Hall of Learning at the love vigils and demanding them, yet still remaining blind and deaf, and with the overwhelming sense of solitude. It is probable, if they thoroughly examine themselves, that the attributes which are a part of human character, and are developed in human life, are still not fully attained. These are discernment, reason, justice, and honor. Until these are attained, the disciple cannot enter upon psychic experience, for his development must be perfect and equal, as are the petals of the lotus flower; and his nature must open itself according to the true law, balanced and complete, as the bud of the perfect flower opens. Therefore psychic consciousness cannot come to him till he is ready to use it rightly. If a man who becomes a disciple, desiring to tread the true path of development, has had psychic consciousness, and is without the perfect moral balance required, his first bitter experience will be the loss of these inner senses. They are taken from him because of the danger involved in their possession until he has passed through the severe preparations and ordeals. This is the simple explanation of the difference between the psychic gifts of the occultist and of the spiritualist. Those who are called by the name "spiritualist," seize upon the gifts without the necessary preparation, and may be, in their psychic bodies, among either good or evil companions. The disciple, when his psychic senses are opened, finds himself in his own place, in his own school. He does not wander in the highways and byways of astral life, which are as full of danger and evil as those of earth; he has to fill his post, to do his appointed work, to stay unwaveringly in that post, and do that work without pause. And it is when he is sufficiently advanced for this that he becomes aware of the presence of those members of the school who are near to him, in the mystic sense—his true companions.

"Where two or three are gathered together, there am I in the midst of them."

Where two or three companions in love become aware of each other, they perceive also the sublime Figure, standing close in their midst, of the One among the Avatars who promised to stay with us even to the end of the world. He has never left us, nor will; in the ethereal spaces He moves among suffering men, becoming visible to them in their moments of extreme agony. In the psychic world He is among the disciples, ceaselessly helping spirits to rise upward, and showing to us the way, the truth, and the life. Many times must the disciple pass through the ordeals and purifications of the whole mystic year before the recognition of the "two or three" is possible. This is not necessary in order to see the Christ. He came to publicans and sinners, and He comes to them still; the only qualification needed is that of utter repentance, or of extremest suffering. But to see, and hear, and feel the other two or three, and be aware of the Figure in the midst, is possible only for one who is able to stand firmly in his place, and who cannot be cast down from it.

Many, very many, disciples are present at the later Ceremonies year after year, without the power to enter upon the ordeals or to attempt to pass the initiations. They gather strength and knowledge from being witnesses of the mystic rites. These trials are beyond the capacity of solitary spirits, still subject to the illusion of separateness. Only when recognition between the true companions has taken place in the psychic life can full initiation become possible. None can lift the heavy iron bar alone. When first the illusion of separateness weakens its hold, an overwhelming sense of solitude falls upon the disciple; for those whom he encounters, or is surrounded by, upon the physical plane, are not likely to be his true companions, and if they were he would not be able to recognize them with the physical senses. He is warned that this spiritual association may not be looked for in

any external love or friendship, however deep
and pure these may be. Whoever looks for
it within a physical attraction turns his attention in the wrong direction, and this
brings its own punishment. It is only in the
occult ceremonies and vigils that the recognition of spiritual comrades can take place. If,
when the consciousness comes to you of those
who are your true companions, you find one
who is a friend on earth, then may you know
that you have gone far indeed upon the path.
To be powerful enough to attain association
with a companion on the physical as well as
on the psychic plane means that the divine
part of the man has been able to unfold a
petal of its lotus flower and to permit its
sweetness to become a fragrance that can
reach the outer sense. For this wonderful
thing must come from on high; it means that
two initiates are fated or permitted to meet
upon earth—a marvel in an aeon. None but
a high initiate knows how to test the bond
between friends, and ascertain its true character, in the outer consciousness.

## CHAPTER V

No one who has once seen the whiteness at the Feast of Love, can ever rest again in the sloth of indifference in which men are plunged, and in which many disciples linger. This is henceforth impossible. The heart opens itself even to those whose deeds make them a pain and weariness even to think of. When a disciple has attended the Feast of Love many times, has passed its ordeals and penetrated into its mysteries, then the blaze of color disappears, the crimson of passion and the flame of desire are gone, and all is white as the lily. When the disciple sees this, he may know that he has entered the first degree of the white brotherhood, which exists within the body of love, its core and center. Then comes the surpassing wonder of the voice of the silence, which comes softly and mysteriously, like a pulse beating a little more loudly than before and by slow and strange progress becomes definite and clear. It does not come as a miraculous sound penetrating to the intelligence on rare occasions, but as a constant guide and dictator. By its means, orders reach the spirit of the man, and are understood by his material intelligence in such a manner that he not only knows how to obey them, but knows that they have to be obeyed, just as certainly and absolutely as the laws of Nature have to be obeyed. Personal orders reach him, and he is taught the details of the advanced disciple's life, without need of any external master to guide him. He is told how to maintain the required daily concentration for an unbroken period during the six sacred months, how to witness the mystic ceremonies and feasts while still unable to endure their ordeals, how to make himself a part of the great drama, and enter into its tragic progress, though not yet an initiate. When this difficult task has been perfectly fulfilled once, the next year he may hope to lift the heavy iron bar and enter fully into the ceremonies, and pass with safety, though with suffering, through the ordeals.

Even should the one who has seen the whiteness wish to give up the battle and be again as those who care not, it will be an impossibility. Once opened, even though only to the extent of a single petal, the flower can never return to the state of being a bud. The spirit has been awakened, and must strive and work on upon its appointed course, without any rest or intermission but that of the deep consciousness which keeps the spirit safe during fret and turmoil; this blessed refreshment is now its own by right, for in its depths it has become aware of the awful, infinite repose. With the awakening of the spirit has come the marvelous consciousness of surrounding presences, of a united army, whose members stand close together, bound, not by rule or command, but by the beating of all hearts together, by the one desire that fills all spirits, by the oneness of the aim which animates all.

The undeveloped members of the human race are wrapped in an illusion, and move in it as men move in a fog; it causes them to imagine that each one of their race is a separate being, able to act alone, and to grasp all that is good and valuable in life for himself, if only he is sufficiently strong and determined, and absolutely selfish. What a palpable delusion this is to anyone who looks a little way beyond the outline of his own shape! Regard, but for a moment, the ebb and flow of Nature, and you find that outline is but a temporary and impermanent part of it, ceaselessly changing and interchanging. Separation of the body from it surroundings, were it possible, would mean death. So with the spirit. It is never separated from its spiritual surroundings; it is only an illusion that the material shape isolates it. Therefore is it that the spirit of man does not require to do aught but awaken to the realities of his being, and attain to full consciousness. Then, once more, all is his; the illimitable spaces, the worlds of spiritual life, the heart of love, which is the hearth of the world, where all

come in due course to find warmth and infinite comfort.

Remember that the animal soul in man,
and the divine spirit in him, cannot be in full
activity at the same time. One must be in
abeyance.

With the man of the world it is the divine
spirit in him that is in abeyance. Each man
chooses for himself which is to predominate,
and which is to grow and wax strong as a
giant, while the other becomes fainter and
less active, and less capable of action. His
choice will be that of true desire. None other
is of any use. Slaves have no place among the
disciples, nor can they enter among them. He
who decides to go upon the high path, does
so because he desires to, and his suffering becomes to him as joy; and thus he enters into
ecstasy. Then comes the strange knowledge
that pleasure and pain are but two aspects
of one thing, though to the ordinary man
they seem to be utterly and absolutely disso-
ciated, wide apart as the poles.

Hold your animal soul still, while you talk
with your divine self; put your foot on it, and

compel it to serve you; but do not attempt
to kill it before its time. It will only come to
life again, and confront you suddenly, in a
new shape, filling you with dismay and fear.
You have not the power to kill it. Your way
of escape from it is to make it your servant,
to transform its powers into divine forces,
and to transfer your interest to those. In
working this miracle, all the subtle and beneficent powers of earth and heaven will silently, yet resolutely, aid you, because you
will be obeying their laws. The ascetic opposes the laws both of Nature and super-
Nature, and so becomes an outcast and an
alien, and has to fight alone, and stumble
helplessly along a hopeless road. He is a fore-
doomed failure, for none who walks alone
can hope to lift the iron bar.

Having considered the physical fact of non-
separateness, what you must then remember
is that Nature and super-Nature work on
analogous lines, and under laws of corre-
spondences. All laws become more marked,
more positive, and more inexorable in the
greater life than in the lesser, in super-Nature

than in Nature. While on the threshold of occult life, it is necessary to have faith in order to move in the right direction, for super-Nature is unknown and invisible. But once the spiritual consciousness is awakened within you, and the psychic senses opened, you will realize and recognize the law of non-separateness immediately. Look around you and note the melting, fusing power of actual spiritual life! See how the teacher's consciousness becomes that of the pupil, how the lover's soul becomes that of the loved, how the mother and child interchange thought without speech. The greatest love of all, greater than all these, is the love of the Master for his disciple. He is father and mother, lover and friend, to the one who is learning, who leans toward him, and who has entered into that body of love of which he himself is a part.

When once the sense of separateness has been removed, the greatest obstacle to the path of power is removed. Its dangers are removed also. For when the man has reached this stage of advancement, he is become utterly selfless, and all power that is his is used for the whole, not for himself. "That power which the disciple shall covet is that which shall make him appear as nothing in the eyes of men." This is the rule, written in flaming words, that shall last as long as the world lasts, on the wall of the Hall of Learning.

Man can rebuild his physical nature, and create his divine nature out of it, only when he knows that neither it, nor the animating power within it, are his own, or are even himself. When he knows this, he is ready to build his body anew, and form within it a spiritual shape worthy of immortality.

While he regards himself as apart from others, even from any whose sin he loathes, or whose hatred he has incurred, while he has any desire for himself, even the desire of rest or of quiet, so long is he blind and dumb and helpless in the presence of the Great Ones.

Human love ends with human life; therefore is it necessary to know and experience it to the full, for its lessons are a part of the experience of the pilgrimage of man. The love, the satisfaction, the sense of union that

come beyond human life are inexpressibly
sweeter and stronger than any human emotion; but through human emotions they must
be reached. There is no other road for men.
Then the knowledge gained by love satisfied
has become a part of the man, and joy and
grief are no longer distractions, but have become something else, united in a new emotion which will remain with him always. The
myrtle, the little tree of personal life, has
grown to its full height, and reached its
flowering time, and looked into the heavens
with the eyes of its flowers. Now it lies low,
a scented carpet in the temple of devotion.

Spiritual love is the atmosphere, or rather,
the spiritual ether, in which the spiritual
spheres revolve and move in their appointed
paths. When the spirit is aware of this, and
familiar with the knowledge, its spiritual activity commences. That which is called love
in ordinary human language, the passion
which is awakened by the contact of two per-
sonalities, is not merely the means by which
the generations come upon the earth. Men,
whose sight and knowledge are limited to

things material, think this is so. But those who have lifted but a little way the iron bar which fastens the gates of gold, know well that the passion which by men is called love has another and a greater use than even the creation of life in this world. It also creates life in the world beyond. It is the stepping-stone from earth to heaven, from the things of matter to the things of spirit. All touch it, more or less, sooner or later; the most hard-ened human being has some feeling for some other being—it may be love for an old mother or a helpless child. There is a chink in the armor of selfishness to be found in all, and the experience arising from it is as inev-itable as birth or death. Like them, it may be a seemingly barren effort, scarcely worth recording on the sands of time; or it may grow into something splendid, marking the awakening of a soul into its great heritage, the life of spiritual love. The man to whom passion remains only passion remains only man. For him the earth will continue to re-volve, and the sun to shine, so long as he needs these things; for him the green leaves will come forth yearly upon the trees, without meaning; the springtide will utter its resurrection message, and he will know nothing of it.

The bitterness of life and its experiences, and of contact with those who live in hatred, and whose spirits are blind and deaf, makes the hearts of men like the trees in wintertime, dark and dry. Did we not see the miracle of the green leaves take place yearly, we could not believe in it when looking upon a frost-bound earth. But the learned gardener has seen the tiny purple and brown promises of buds, before the frost came, and knows they are safely hidden beneath it, kept warm by the subtle earth-life that feeds the growing plants. So with the hearts of men. The Master, the initiate, wise in the lore of human nature, a gardener of men, watches them pass through bitter ordeals that seem like spiritual death, knowing full well a bud of life is hidden within, which will burst forth when the bitterness is over and past.

Man must die; yet the loss of a loved one by death is the heaviest loss life has for us.

But wait! Over the memory of the dead friend a mystic greenness grows, as a natural greenness grows over his grave; and in the future a new friend may hold your hand and talk to you of him, and by his words and thoughts make the greenness grow thicker. Both may be your true companions, and, if so, you cannot be parted from them; if they are not, parting from both is inevitable. In the brave heart, the strong soul, love reawakens triumphantly, and puts forth its resolute green leaves—like the green leaves of Nature, soft, delicate, fragile, easily plucked or crushed, yet unconquerable in their recurrent life and beauty. And the disciple, knowing that love gives and asks not, loves unceasingly the one that has gone far away as well as the one that is with him.

The emotions of the heart—passions, jealousies, hopes, and fears—which overwhelm men from time to time, may drive them to fever, and from fever to madness. When this occurs, it is because men are blind and ignorant, and do not know how to build up, out of themselves, divine beings. They are unaware that each drop of blood in the body of a man can be changed in its nature and become a part of his spiritual being; and that this transformation and transmutation is required of him. Every power and every passion possessed by man is his by divine intent, and when he crushes out or neglects any part of his nature, he is false to his trust. Out of the natural being the spiritual being must arise, fully equipped, and perfected in shape.

It is the emotions which admit you to the citadel of the soul; it is through the heart that you reach yourself.

It is by transforming the emotions that the fever of life is cured, and its madness cast aside.

Transform all feeling into power.

Take emotion and make it purpose.

Take fever and make it force.

Take madness and make it divine confidence.

# FEBRUARY AND MARCH
## Human Life and Human Death
### The Ceremony of Life and Death
#### 21st March

# CHAPTER VI

*H*ow are these transformations to be effected? The month of February is devoted to a vigil of preparation, during which three steps have to be taken. In certain psychic schools the month is divided into three periods of nine days each. These steps mean, respectively, the attaining of self-control, self-reliance, and obedience. In studying and attaining these, the mystery of the love teaching becomes intelligible.

Life is starred by strange moments, which differ from all the rest of time by reason of the fact that great decisions have to be made in them, decisions which can only be dealt with by the higher self. When these moments arrive, the man is either entirely helpless before them, or else he realizes at once that now no mundane or ordinary considerations can weigh the balance. The events of life, unfolding out of each other with all the silent mystery of natural growth, lead a man by imperceptible and subtle progress to one of these great moments, and he finds himself constrained to make a decision of such a character that his whole being is compelled to take part in the struggle. The man who is helpless before these trials yields to feeling and emotion, becomes a prey to fever and to madness. The disciple stands unshaken on the battlefield of his nature, in the midst of the turmoil of life, and resolutely effects the transmutation within himself. The feeling within him, the agony of emotion which an intense situation in human life has called into existence, can be changed into power, and used to a great end. The highest motive he can see or reach to must be his guide, that and none other; the most selfless action possible must be the one of his choice. If he adheres unflinchingly to this standard, suddenly he will find the fever within him abate, while those around him will be sensible of a force emanating from him, which leads them also upward, and compels them to follow the highest motives known to them. Then the despair and misery, which will be capable of producing madness in men not so led and guided, will suddenly turn to confidence in the unseen and beneficent powers, and out of a vortex of passion, or a sea of suffering, the spirits of those involved in it will arise purified. This is the task of the disciple in daily life and human intercourse, by which great effort he transforms evil into good in the lives of those around him. All life becomes thought, when dealt with in this manner, for there is no event so simple that it does not contain a lesson for the student. There is no detail in daily life too trivial to be treated in this manner; some events cannot be met in any other way.

This period in the year illustrates and typifies man's experience between birth and death. That life-experience, which seems to the ignorant to be all that man is, and all that he has, is in truth only the preparation for physical death and the transmutation which should follow it, and which does follow it when the disciple is sufficiently prepared. This long vigil, with its daily prayers and meditations, is maintained from the time when the birth ceremonies are completed to the time when the celebration of the Crucifixion is reached. At this strange and deeply mysterious hour, throughout Christendom the idea of the Man upon the Cross is present to all minds. It was the special work of the Christ to show forth and make plain the meaning of the Cross, a symbol which has existed from all time, and has been but dimly understood. It was the task of the last Avatar to raise it high before men's eyes, and plant it in their hearts. Man, crucified in time and space, is that which results from the birth of spirit into matter. In the psychic world the spirit of the disciple endures the higher crucifixion of suffering with, and in, the whole human race, as the Christ Himself still suffers. The little child has come into being and obtained that which it demanded; has grown strong enough to suffer, and must now endure to the uttermost the pain of that condition which we call life—physical life, or psychic life.

The disciple has now concentrated his attention upon the Ceremonies and Feasts of Birth, which symbolize his willing descent into matter and his entrance upon human life; he has perhaps witnessed the Ceremonial of these. Should he have endured all their ordeals, he will have passed beyond such guidance as can be given here.

The one ordeal which he has certainly endured is that which accompanies the desire of birth.

None can enter upon the litanies of the Crucifixion, or attempt to lead the Christ life, until he has taken the three steps toward perfections which are taught at this period.

The Master, who explained the meaning of the Cross and gave fragments of the ritual for the initiation to the Christ life to His disciples, preached no asceticism or aloofness from men, for He knew that the necessary ordeals are endured in human life. For this, human life exists. The mystic and occult ritual is exemplified and fulfilled in the daily life of the world—the very purpose of this daily life being the awakening and purifying of the spirit of man, which is only possible through the heart and its emotions. The steps which must be taken before these emotions can be even dimly understood, instead of blindly felt, are these three.

Self-control is recognized as the first requirement for the man who is ambitious. To the disciple, who essays a greater thing than any that is aimed at by the ambitious man, it means the control of the lower self so that it obeys the dictates of the higher. The self-control taught by ambition is as an armor or shield to protect the man from other men. It does no concern itself with the inner state of the man. The permanent benefit which is obtained from it is that of strength. The self-control taught in the mystic life is that which involves the purification of the heart. It is the control of the lower self, the manhood, by the higher self, the warrior. This can only be attained by one whose direction is fixed, who knows that he desires spiritual development rather than any other thing whatever, and who knows this always, without any shadow of turning. The lower self must not be killed, for it is as a root in the earth from which will spring a great tree. It must follow the laws of all natural life—grow, and become strong, and then become exhausted by experience; being throughout under absolute control.

During the period known as human life, that which is human love should attain to its fullness, and be complete ere it is laid aside. It is by the conquest of the lower self in the intense experiences of love and grief, joy and anguish, effort and disaster, success and failure, that the miracle of transmutation is effected in man's nature. There is no other way, for the path leads through human life to the life beyond it. When one separates himself from humanity, he leaves the path, he turns aside, and his steps must be retraced. For the purpose of experiencing human emotions and learning from them, do the spirits of men descend into matter, and become crucified in time and space. This is the meaning of the time-old symbol of the Cross, which

appeared first without the Figure, symboliz-
ing the mystery of creation, time and space,
and all the conditions of material life, having been made ready. Then the Figure appears, entering consciously upon its suffering
in the experience of life within the limitations
of the pairs of opposites. As the Svastika, the
Cross is found on Chaldean bricks; in ancient
Egypt it appeared in the ansated form; the
Spanish conquerors of Mexico found it used
there, and designated "The Tree of Our
Life"; it has been discovered on the backs of
the gigantic statues found on the submerged
continent in the mid-Pacific Ocean; it is the
oldest symbol in India. The Egyptian deities
carried the ansated Cross as a symbol of the
god in man; with the Figure came the idea
of the Deity suffering as man, and suffering
consciously, enduring the crucifixion which
is man's lot, for love of man.

Those who live through their human life
with the sole object of obtaining pleasure and
avoiding pain, refusing to take the step of ac-
quiring self-control, not only retrace their
course until they can follow it rightly, but

find experience more and more intensified, the torture more defined and acute. For man, if he will not learn, must be taught. Through incarnation after incarnation the unwilling students are compelled to learn, by severity of trial and misfortune.

## CHAPTER VII

*T*he second step, the attainment of self-reliance, compels the disciple to call upon
the warrior—his own higher self. The man
who acquires self-reliance in the experience
of daily life can trust to the guidance of his
intellect or of his animal soul, either being
capable of dealing with selfish interests to the
advantage of the self. But the disciple has to
decide on questions which have to do with
the good of others, with the good of the all;
and he is compelled to do so without help
from his teacher, or any guidance save that
of the light of the Logos within himself, in
order that he shall acquire self-reliance.

The animal soul of man, illumined only by
intellect, enters into the arena of life as a wild

beast goes forth to secure its prey, and following only the instincts of attack and self-preservation. Led by it, the spirit finds itself tossed hither and thither, fighting desperately for that which is worthless when obtained, herding with the herd, and with the hopeless ones who kill or are killed, according to the fortunes of war, without object and without meaning.

Look for the Warrior now, and listen to him when he cries, "This is but a struggle for broken toys—this is no part of the great preparation."

The whole of human life becomes to the disciple a conscious preparation for that which will follow it, only when he has passed through his allotted experiences from the pairs of opposites, has suffered from all the pangs of incompleteness and warfare, has been both man and woman, happy and miserable, fortunate and unfortunate, successful and unsuccessful, rich and poor, ruling and ruled. With the lessons and experiences of these opposite conditions garnered in his spiritual memory, and held firmly there as a

priceless possession, he passes through life
again and yet again, watching ceaselessly to
note whether all has been learned. Wherever
the emotions he experiences show him that
the lesson has been incompletely acquired, or
the decisions falteringly made, he resolutely
turns back, and goes again over that step,
seeking another similar incarnation in which
to accomplish it successfully. He is not told
to do this; the repetition would be worthless
if made at the bidding of another, even that
of the highest initiate. The disciple must rely
upon his own judgment, and trust to his own
observation. Also the sacrifice of returning
and retracing his steps must be made willingly, and on his own initiative, not as any
part of obedience. It is because of this retracing of steps that men feel the strange sense
of familiarity which so often comes to them
at high and critical moments of life. Even to
men who have not yet entered upon the path,
this sense comes in desperate hours.
Murderers and suicides feel a frightful familiarity in the frenzied act which they are set
upon, at the moment of accomplishing it.

The various events which drive them to it recede then, and become unimportant, and they are aware of themselves as having taken life before, again and again, because the passion is in them to do so. They have to continue suffering from just such paroxysms of despair, or anger, in other lives, until the higher self takes command and refuses to allow the fatal error to be again committed. Only the man's own higher nature can make this decision, and prevent the utter downfall of the spirit, which means beginning at the very beginning of the whole pilgrimage. Each one who thus falls back delays the emancipation of the whole race. So with the disciple and that body of love to which he belongs. While he is inseparable from that body, yet every atom of it has its own responsibility, and must rely upon itself. When action comes, then is the test; if the highest is always chosen, the spirit remains immovable in its place—fixed, firm, triumphant. He who cannot recognize the highest, or cannot decide to choose it when recognized, wavers and falls aside, and so disorders the whole;

he loses his place, and another, more confident and certain, has to take it.

Now comes the awful test of obedience.

The moments of decision which arrive to the man, and to the disciple, as a climax to a series of events, these come within the domain and power of mankind. There are other far more awful moments when the hand of a supreme power interferes in the affairs of men, and when the man, even though he be a disciple, is helpless. There are decisions made in a court above us all, from which there is no appeal, which are carried out inexorably. Then there is no decision to be made by the man himself; he can only rebel or obey. The religious man calls this supreme power which gives, and takes away, God; occultists see it in the working of the law of Karma. Be it what it may, if the man rebels against it, the disciple may not. It is not for him to blaspheme when he is deprived of his best-beloved or flung violently from a place of peace and apparent usefulness; that is evident. But neither is it for him to ask for help, or pray for relief. When the great power moves, it is for him to obey, and to obey without a murmur even in the secret recesses of his inmost heart. It is by the quality of his obedience that he shows his disciplehood. Resignation is no part of a disciple's equipment. That is left behind, on the path, with peace; left upon steps which he need not retrace, which he will never see again. Resignation is the resource of the philosopher, it is no weapon of the warrior. The soldier who is fit to become a general is the one who endures every hardship and obeys every order, not only without protest, but in perfect confidence that the hardships are necessary and that the order is right. It is not for him to judge; he is only a soldier. He has not the plan of the battle laid out like a map before him; he does not receive messages from distant parts of the field. Therefore, if his beloved friend, perhaps his own son, is suddenly fetched and taken away out of his sight forever, and he may not know his fate, it is not for him to swerve or falter. The general

knows the right place for each soldier; it is
not for the soldiers to judge, either for themselves or those associated with them.

It would seem as if such an ordeal could
only come to the man when grown, and
strong enough to bear pain. But this is not
so. The relationships of human life are so arranged that love and hatred, the great pair
of opposites, make their presence known as
quickly as the inferior pair of heat and cold.
The little child, by its very helplessness, de-
mands love. All who enter as little children
into a new life make that demand. It may
be refused. The unloved child whose presence
is undesired in the family it has entered, the
hated child who causes anger and injury by
its arrival, suffer the high ordeal of learning
obedience. If they survive it without failure,
without becoming embittered and full of hatred themselves, and step forth later on to
find human beings who give them love, it is
obvious that they have reached this step in
their development, and have been enabled to
pass over it at the beginning of an incarnation, in order to reach it in its higher aspect

in the same lifetime. Doubtless, the rest of their lives may seem to men what is called fortunate. External good fortune and human affection may follow them as they approach the dreadful experience of the higher aspect of this step.

The obedient one must have patience, and the will to endure.

The disciple who has considered these things, and inquired of the earth its secrets, and of the universe its mysteries, knows that there is no reason, save that of the salvation of the race, why men should suffer. There is abundant wealth for all, as there is abundant air for all; love is omnipotent and all-pervading; all organisms are marvelously constructed for pleasure. But the mystic destiny of man necessitates deprivation. Seeing that this is so, his aim becomes that of giving to his obedience its true quality and perfect character.

The greatness of his desire to serve, and to save, opens the door of his sympathy so wide that he perceives, unveiled, the pain of others. He is compelled to exercise the true

obedience in respect to others as well as in
respect to himself. Long after he has conquered rebellion in connection with his own
sufferings, he finds it arise passionately at the
sight of the sufferings of others. This rebellion
will create a darkness round him so that he
cannot help the sufferers. Having become
obedient, it is his mission to help; only the
truly obedient are really able to lift the fallen
and soothe the sick. For only they can do it
rightly, having no canker of rebellion in their
utter sympathy.

The one that is near (in the external, not
in the mystic sense) is the one to whom duty
is owed and to whom help should be given.
The disciple, as well as the ordinary man,
must experience the ordeal of family life—
that device which brings the first nearness to
the materializing spirit. He may be exempt
from some of the later developments common
to most human being, school and college,
business, work, marriage, fatherhood. Never-
theless, though he may be permitted a par-
tial retreat and exemption, in and around all
the circumstances of every day are inter-

woven innumerable threads, drawing souls
of all kinds near to him. Men, children, birds,
and beasts, surround him and must cross his
path. To all who do, he owes the duty of
helping; they have the claim of nearness. Led
by unconscious knowledge, drawn by old
links, now invisible yet plainly felt, beings
come from afar to enter his environment; beings human, sub-human, superhuman. He
must see these suffer; he cannot look away.
He is compelled to exercise the true obedience
while he gives the true love, which gives, but
asks not.

He may not dread loss for himself; if so,
then he must learn to bear it for others. So
much is taken from us during the span of
human life that it would seem as if gifts are
showered upon human beings only to be
taken from them. Youth, beauty, life itself,
are taken from all, even the most fortunate.
All man's possessions may, at any moment,
vanish into the mysterious unseen, and very
often they do so. The man hangs naked on
the Cross, with no cheer, until his spirit tri-
umphs and frees itself. Then he looks round

to find he is in that place to which all that he had has been withdrawn—out of space, out of time, free from the arms of the Cross, and the clash of the pairs of opposites. Youth is an eternal fact, what we call age is the shrinking of the sheath upon the spirit. Beauty retires within the sheath, and adorns the triumphant spirit. Life cries out in its strength, calling to the laggards, who linger in temporary refuges and perishing sheaths, to awaken and enter into it in its fullness.

# CHAPTER VIII

*T*he desire of birth, and the accomplishment of birth, followed by the experiences of love and life, have been the subject of the occult ceremonies and vigils so far. They are the subject of the whole Christmas and New Year celebrations, under all disguises, in all religions, and howsoever veiled and obscured by latter-day tradition. These being completed, it is now necessary for the disciple to turn his attention to the ritual concerning the soul's descent into matter, which was given in Egypt as an esoteric teaching only, for the enlightenment of those who were ready for knowledge. Their great ceremonials and teachings dealt obscurely with the mystery and uses of death, and showed to men how to pass through this change in such a manner as to attain to a higher state of consciousness, and, when rebirth became necessary, to be reborn in higher conditions of life. The object was to show men not only how to live rightly, but how to die rightly. In the mystic teaching of Good Friday and Easter Day, the disciples learned the secrets of their own natures, the meaning of the Fall, and the truth concerning the descent into matter, hidden from ordinary men. Death is itself the greatest teacher, the one universal teacher, on this subject. In the western religions, death is not recognized as a power which loves men and instructs them. It is necessary, therefore, to follow the rule of the esoteric Egyptian ritual, which devoted this part of the period when the sun moves northward to the consideration and study of death, as a fit preparation for the consideration and study of the Tomb itself.

The descent of the spirit of man into matter was the outcome of the need for purification and regeneration. Unless he secures regeneration, and obtains the power to retrace his steps and become reborn again in higher states of being, he will descend too deeply into the Tomb; he will have missed his mark, and risk becoming engulfed altogether. The office of the ministering angel, Death, is to free man from matter temporarily, and to instruct him in his danger. Death is, in fact, a great, conscious, devoted, loving Power which strives ceaselessly to help man to strike off his bonds. No man dies alone, for Death himself is with him; and the dying man finds in him a familiar and most true friend. To the ancient Egyptian, this was known and accepted, and he devoted himself to considering the steps he must take when he passed from his body, and from earth, in the charge of Death.

In the *Devaduta-sutta* (translated by Dr. Oldenburg) is given a conversation between Yama, the God of Death, and the spirit of a wicked man in his charge, in which Yama explains the law of Karma to him, and urges him to take warning. He impresses upon the spirit of the man, strongly, how absolutely responsible he is for his own unfortunate plight. "These, thy evil deeds," says King Yama, "thou alone hast done them all; thou alone must bear the fruit." And the unfortunate one is dismissed into a state of suffering and expiation, instead of becoming the postulant, the Ka of the Egyptians, who is initiated by Death into things divine, and helped by this great Power, between each incarnation, to raise himself higher, and make ready for final emancipation. When that far-off goal shall be reached by the race, then shall the great Power, who waits for us perpetually at the gateway of our human nature, be freed from his task, which claims from him the uttermost devotion.

Those who have not begun to study the mysteries know blindly that physical death lies before them, and that it cannot be avoided; but they do not see what it is, because they do not look upon it. They look away from it, and regard its advent as the coming of an evil hour. The disciple who has begun to look upon this great, wonderful, universal event in the history of man's spirit, knows immediately that it is a good hour

which brings him to it. Whether it is long delayed—postponed to old age—whether it
comes suddenly, whether it comes in youth
or middle age, it is always good. For then the
spirit meets one of its great teachers, one of
its greatest friends. In the case of death he
may rest a while, and learn as to his true
place in the universe, and of his hopes and
opportunities. For, unless he is strong enough
to "proceed to Heaven and kneel among the
stars," to use the words of the postulant in
Chapter XV of the Egyptian Book of the
Dead, he is not urged to do so. He must himself be able to address Ra, and utter the
prayer, "May I proceed as thou dost, without halt, like thy holiness, Ra, thou who hast
no master." Death will hold the helpless one
safely, explain all to him, give him his utmost
opportunity. "I do not think life provides for
all," said Walt Whitman, "but I believe
Heavenly Death provides for all." This was
the faith, or unconscious knowledge, of a
great seer. The philosopher approaches death
with courage, the religious man with hope
or resignation; the man of the world too often

with dismay. The disciple must learn to approach it with knowledge, acquired by looking fearlessly, and with reverence, upon it, and studying that which he perceives. He will soon realize how great a friend awaits him at the end of a life's experience; a friend who has awaited him many times before, and helped him into new places, giving him timely instruction.

During the period when the sun moves southward, it is unwise and unlucky to commence any great effort, according to the Brahmans. Therefore it is now that the contemplation and study of Death must be undertaken, although the autumn and winter belong to King Yama. The Sattras,[1] which are an imitation of the sun's yearly course, are divided into two halves; the ceremonies are in the two halves the same, but they are in the latter half in an inverted order. The Vassa of Buddhism is the time of reciting the law, and was instituted by Buddha in order to prevent the priests from walking over the

---

[1]Brahmanical sacrificial sessions

growing grass which sprang up in the rains. This comes in midsummer, when the "Sailing of the bark of Ra" was celebrated in Egypt. The recitation of the law has been learned, and the observance of daily duties, is, after this, all that is possible until the birth month again returns, and Light again arrives in the form of a little child. Now is the time to endeavor to look steadily towards the abyss which awaits all men, and to learn that a great angel truly stands there always, stretching out helping hands to the spirits of men.

In order to see death, it is necessary to pass into the deep concentration in which it is possible to approach the hearth of the material universe where temporal fires are lit from the great flame. The Nature Spirit, which works side by side with the Spirit of Love throughout the ages, stands upon the hearth, sometimes within the flame of the human desire of life, sometimes outside it. Here stands Death also.

In order to approach the hearth of life, it is necessary to concentrate first upon the mystery of all flames and fires.

The great fire all see, and which we call the sun, the unseen fire in the heart of the earth, have been mystically lit and are mystically preserved, tended unceasingly by their ministers. Innumerable fires are thus tended, many of which do not concern man at all. But never are the fires that enable men to live, forgotten. They keep Death at bay, so that he takes his harvest of lives one at a time, save in special cases. Were the fires not tended continually, did they not send forth their flames with ceaseless vigor, the whole human race would fall into the arms of Death, in one dreadful moment of time, and time itself would end. In the dimness of the remote future, when the pilgrimage of man is accomplished, the fires will go out. Why do the ministers tend them so tirelessly? It is for the disciple to ask of the Holy Ones their secrets. Only they can answer, to each man's spirit.

The province of Death is to release the spirits of men from crucifixion in the flesh. To all just men he comes as an opener of prison doors, one who lets in the light. At the least, for those who, though blind, have been just, he releases them into the Elysian fields where there is rest and pleasure. But this is no greater freedom than to come out of a house into its garden, if you have not the power to go beyond the garden and must needs presently return, if not into the same house, yet into one like it. Death asks more of his charges than this, and he continually instructs them as to the mode of reaching a higher place. Unjust men are ushered by Death into places of horror, and there is little to be wondered at in the fear of Death which haunts some men all their lives. It is born of bitter experience and subconscious memory. For Death, friend of man though he is, can find no easy or quiet place for the wicked man.

It is the conquest of the desires of the outer senses which gives to the disciple the right to inquire of the Holy Ones of their secrets. None can truly see Death till his eyes are the eyes of the regenerate, when tears can never again be shed for any grief or loss or pain. This can therefore only be possible when grief and pain have been endured and exhausted, in successive incarnations, and the disciple is far upon the path. Those who look towards Death intelligently, yet see not, persevere in the task they have entered upon, knowing that sight will come later. And then they will find themselves in harmony with that which they wish to see. This is a part of the occult truth, discovered and declared by Tolstoy, that in the life of the spirit, *direction* is all-important. The unseeing yet resolute one, pressing on in the dark by the guidance of his highest aspirations, will open his eyes one day on beauty and light unimaginable, and find himself surrounded by great and powerful friends, towards whom he has found his way with difficulty, yet unerringly, because his direction has been rightly made by the guidance of his higher self.

The experience of death, which comes to every man, is not in itself a preparation for the great Good Friday ceremony. It is only by looking straight upon Death, and asking of him his secrets, that the passing into his

charge becomes a preparation. He will answer you, be sure; and instead of explaining
to you, as to the ordinary man, that law of
Karma of which he is one of the administra-
tors, he will enter upon a different and much
more difficult discourse. He will show you
the nature of matter, and what its power is
over the spirit of man, and he will prepare
you for the mystery of the Tomb. The disciple who has not attained sight can only demand it ceaselessly, and continue to direct his
unseeing gaze towards that which he longs
to know and understand. Much will be un-
folded to him and made intelligible while he
thus perseveres, and order will appear in the
seeming chaos by which he is surrounded. He
perceives plainly that there is no such thing
as chance or accident; that Death, working
within the area where the fires are kept burning for the protection of man, can take only
those lives which are surrendered to him.
Gradually he will begin to recognize the coming and presence of Death, before the physical event takes place which goes by its name,

and will feel it lingering after that is over. A strong and solemn atmosphere belongs to it, which changes the aspect of all things.

To the ordinary man, who seeks no such experiences as these, the profound abyss of grief is that place of consciousness in which he first becomes dimly aware of the stately presence that is so near to him. He suddenly recognizes that what is happening is not only the loss of one close to him, but that there is a new and great presence, benign and beautiful, pressing upon him. As he contemplates it, he experiences the sensation of being blessed; from the presence of death comes a profound good-will to man.

None can make this great essay, of taking the knowledge of death and learning the mysteries that lie hid in its keeping, who has not been perfectly obedient to the simple rule, "Thou shalt not kill." Man hinders his progress on the path by arrogating to himself rights which are not his. The Buddha taught men explicitly that they had no right to take life, but mankind has not yet begun to learn the lesson. The disciple is told to respect life

as those do who desire it. The knowledge of
death is utterly hidden from those who do not
realize its sacredness. The disciple has to
understand the lesson of Buddha, that life in
itself is sacred, a sacred possession of the one
to whom it has been given, whether human
or animal. It is for the preservation of this
gift that the great flames are lit and tended.
When one regards the midges in the sunshine,
it seems as though life is so abundant that it
cannot be intrinsically of value. That is an
illusion, born of the conditions of time and
space, which confuse the true sense of values.
Life is both precious and sacred to the small-
est thing that dances in the air, or hides in
the earth, no matter for how brief a time it
may possess that life. Buddha and Christ
have both taught this. How have their so-
called followers fulfilled their behests? The
solemn and beautiful presence of Death
comes in its majesty equally at the end of the
little fluttering life which lasts but a few
hours as to the death-bed of a king, because
every spirit which casts aside its physical
sheath is in his charge. These great forces,

Life and Death, two of the powerful pairs of opposites, remain unalterably splendid. No sordidness of human conditions, no briefness or insignificance of the creature's span of life, can alter the splendor of the possession, or the dignity of that which takes it away, or rather, which transforms it. For Death, in his true province, is not a destroyer but a transformer, one who by a magic touch changes all things. He is also a silencer. His work is to help the spirit of man to freedom, to end his crucifixion, and to still the ceaseless clash and vibration which exists in time and space. But for the tending of the fires, the power of Death would quickly silence the turmoil of the material universe. His power is over material things only; he causes their movement to cease. He can but bless and instruct the spirit of man, and guide him to that place to which his Karmic conditions entitle him. To the ordinary man, he explains the law of Karma. To the disciple, who is duly prepared, he reveals the profound mystery of the blending of one of the great pairs of opposites, and the marvelous thing which arises from that blending. He shows to the disciple that he is both Death and Life to the occultist. It lies with the one who is enduring the initiation to take Death and make it Life. The God of Death lends himself willingly to this transformation, which gives to him the joy of success and accomplishment. For man becoming so great as to be able to do this is the object for which this Power serves with such ceaseless devotion.

The whole meaning and mystery of occultism lie in this magical process of transformation and transmutation. Whilst the disciple is slowly undergoing his purification in the fierce crucible of life, he is at the same time engaged in transforming and transmuting that which is around him. The two processes proceed at the same time, the one inevitably producing the other. With every Ceremony witnessed, every vigil observed, every ordeal endured, the disciple changes not only himself but the world in which he lives. He helps the great Powers towards their release from service to man, and he helps men around him in every crisis of life. His knowledge of death as being life, emanates from him without any need of speech, and helps others in critical and terrible moments of human suffering.

On 21st March, the day on which the sun shines exactly on the equator, when the whole material earth is assured of its annual rebirth into full life, the ceremony of the vigil of death is observed by the disciples. To the "one who walks," birth and death are the two parts of one action. An incarnation is a footstep in the sands of time. Sometimes the foot sinks so deeply into the sand that it is difficult to withdraw it at all, and the spirit is engulfed, and struggles for ages before it can recover itself, and walk as one walks who knows the direction in which he is going. Many experience this disaster and this difficulty; they cling to others in the same way that those do who in material life sink into a slough. Those who can walk, hold out to them helping hands. From this arises the formation of schools of teaching. They exist in order that the spirits of men shall not be delayed too long upon the pilgrimage by such disasters. Those who are wandering aimlessly to and fro in the sands of time, blinded by the mists of matter, are shown a path, and urged to enter upon it and find the Way. They are not always ready to take the path shown to them, for it is uphill, and it is hard. The lethargy born of failure is upon them, and they prefer to linger idly in the darkness, where there is no safety or certainty. It is the task of the few, who have found the hope and security which await those who enter on the path, to call to the ones who linger behind, and draw them onward and upward. With the knowledge that Death and Life are one comes the knowledge that the desire for destruction belongs to the spirit of hatred. Death is no destroyer; he is a turmoil, and gives new life. It is not for man to arrogate to himself the rights of the beneficent Power. In this lies one of those contradictions which are an essential part of the mysteries. Death itself is blessed, but it is not within man's province to give that blessing. When he kills, he makes himself accursed. Death transforms the ill deed for the victim, but he cannot do so for the sinner. The greatest theft of all has been committed, and must be suffered for. The spiritual law has been broken, and one who transgresses the spiritual law remains a transgressor though all the beneficent Powers should unite to transform the effect of his deed, and though the effect of his deed be transformed.

# APRIL
## Good Friday and Easter Day

## CHAPTER IX

With April comes the glorious idea of resurrection. The disciple leaves the dim and sad places in which he has been keeping vigil, and moves into the splendor. He is ready now to devote himself entirely to the contemplation of the most superb conception known to man. The Easter season is the ecstasy of the year, culminating in the great Feast of Resurrection, celebrated throughout Christendom on Easter Day. Then follows the purely spiritual and occult vigil of transmutation, after which the disciple, retaining firmly the place he has reached while the sun moved northward, repeats and recites the lessons he has learned, resolutely aiming at being born into a still higher state

113

of spiritual life when again the birth month is reached.

The Easter season perpetually illustrates and commemorates that freedom which will be obtained by man at the end of his pilgrimage, when he has acquired all the knowledge to be obtained by human experience, and has cast off the last vesture or sheath of the spirit. When that freedom is obtained, the spirit will have finally left the Tomb—risen from the grave—and matter will know it no more.

At the commencement of this great Feast of Resurrection, the Hall of Learning is full of life and activity. The Teachers await their disciples, looking with hope for those whom they have prepared, trusting that they will have the courage to embark on this great enterprise. This is no longer any warfare on that battlefield where the Arjuna of the *Bhagavad Gita* fights his lower nature and his evil passions. That battle has long since been fought and won by the disciple who is strong enough to enter upon the Easter feast, and take his place in the Hall of Learning. This wonderful palace of wisdom was built, and is preserved in the ethereal space that is within reach of the spirits of men, by the initiates who are followers of the Christ, and remain near the world of men to teach and help them. All are bidden to come here, all are helped to enter; but only a few are able to do so. Those who can pass through the doors at this season feel the divine airs, and become aware of the Great Presences. Quick-growing grasses spring up about their footsteps as they enter; all is green around them. It is the time of green leaves; of the opening of buds. Once they are within the doors, the Hall appears to them as vast as the surface of the world itself; for the great invitation to all to come makes the walls recede till there is room for the spirits of all men to stand within them. On all sides are groups and processions of priests, wearing the robes of the world's religions. All alike chant the resurrection hymn. Many of the priests who do office at this season have become enlightened during the preparatory vigils. Some of the worshipers, who have blindly sought the way and earnestly prayed for guidance, are led into the mystic precincts. Those who have intelligently observed the vigil of death are able to hear the chanting of the Good Friday litany. A few, each year, are able to take part in it for the first time. All through the Easter season this glorious litany is maintained ceaselessly by triumphant voices.

I. *I see Death.*
II. *I know Death.*
III. *I am Death.*
IV. *I am Alive.*
V. *I am dead; I am alive.*
VI. *The Divine says: I am that which is evil.*
VII. *The Spirit says: I am that which is matter.*

The whole object of the preparation and suffering lies in this miracle of transformation and transmutation. Here is the supreme mystery to be entered into by the disciple while he remains man. Destroy no thing, but make all things good, all things beautiful, all things desirable. Remember that hate is the destroyer, love the creator and builder. Take

death and make it life, as you take evil and
make it good. The divine cannot be tarnished
by evil any more than gold can suffer by contact with fire. Spirit can no more become
matter than water can become one with fire.
Gold is purified by burning, and the divine
does but throw aside all that is not absolutely itself. As it passes through the fiery ordeal,
Spirit, when it identifies itself with matter,
sweeps it away as water obliterates fire. It
must long to become one with the fire, before
the miracle can be accomplished. The spiritual part of the man must so recognize the
darkness and death of the physical, must so
completely and willingly enter into it and
transform it, the inevitable ill, into a thing
desirable, that it shall dissolve away, and
vanish in its character and quality as that
which is ill or evil. So, in entering the Tomb,
the Christ of the world, the Buddha of the
world, the Krishna of the world, destroys the
Tomb itself. His supreme spirituality is
stronger than that which would hold or bind
him, and his supreme Love changes its nature
into that which does not hold or bind.

And so, after the deep silence of the hours (or ages) of effort, of abasement, the grave yields up its dead, and that which is dead is alive.

It is useless to attempt to understand the true meaning of resurrection until the previous ceremonies have not only been entered into, and fully understood, but their ordeals endured. In this manner, the story of the year follows the story of the life of the ego, the "one who walks." Until the winter is experienced and endured, the green leaves do not come. Until the lessons of human life have been learned, that which lies beyond it is unapproachable. A formidable series of ceremonies and ordeals has been hinted at, and superficially surveyed, in the course of this treatise. Each and all of these must have been fully entered into and understood, grasped from within, not surveyed from without, before the disciple can be more than a witness of the marvelous Feast of the Resurrection. Until then, he can but kneel and pray, and strive to see. It is the sad lot of many disciples, who have believed themselves ready to take part in the Easter Feast, to find that they are unable even to witness it. The glory of the miracle is too great for them to endure to gaze upon it, and the possibility of taking part in it is altogether out of their reach. None cast them forth, for the disciple's right and privilege is that of endurance to the uttermost. But when the splendor becomes blinding, the spirit falls back into the refuge of darkness, and no hands stretched out to help, no call from the master, can prevent this. Then the way has to be recommenced and trodden again, and perhaps yet retrodden, until the wayfarer is able to discover with certainty where he has made the false step, and to pass over that point without fault.

This ecstasy of the year is the true awakening hour of the spirit, when man knows the mystery of love in its fullness, if he is able to take part in the ceremonial. The disciples who enter range themselves like brethren, those who are near each other in the occult sense standing side by side, and pressing together. The infinite spirit love passes through the ranks of its army like a shape of light, and yet it is a thing solid and eternal.

Those who have passed through the Easter Ceremony once can never hurt or kill or give pain any more; and with each season that they pass through it, do they penetrate more and more fully into its glorious depths; they grow in strength, and become vital and irresistible forces in the world. For they have more and more of the power of the united army to use, with every advance they make.

In the deep place of the animal soul is darkness; it is conscious only of material things, of passions and desires. There is no knowledge in it, even of the phenomena of earth life, save by the help of the senses. These are not inalienable possessions, as are the psychic senses of the spirit, which may be closed by the action of the law of Karma, but can never be taken away. The physical senses can be entirely destroyed, so that the animal soul and its instrument, the brain, are left without any information as to outer things. But it is in this deep place of the soul

that the spirit sits shrouded, and it is here that
is the quick spring of love and life eternal.
Here, within every man, is the Tomb, the
place of darkness where the miracle takes
place, from which the spirit rises, in which
the spring of life and love bursts forth. Taste
of this spring, bathe in it, asking no questions,
but simply drinking of it, and the hunger for
knowledge and longing for light will pass
away. These desires of the spirit, which fill
it with restless craving, will pass away, because illumination will have been attained.

The water of life will so gush forth that you
must give of it to others, and in so doing, an
unutterable joy will arise within you. You
have now all that you need and more;
enough for others; enough for all the world.
You have achieved the miracle of the resurrection, you have made the greenness spring
forth within yourself; and in so doing, you
are making the earth green about you, and
bringing the joy of new life upon the world.
In the school of love there is a pledge to be
taken at the very door, before you can enter.

This pledge, already taken in the ordeal of
the Feast of Love, must be said in the heart
of the disciple at the Easter Feast.

"I will Love."

You no longer desire love, or ask love, or
look for love. You give it.

# CHAPTER X

The Master is the servant of humanity, and obeys the demand of the disciple. At the Easter season he awaits those who call on him, within the doors of the Hall of Learning. For it lies with the spirit of the man to arise and step out and forth, and to enter the places of illumination. That which is known as the Hall of Learning stands first outside the gate of matter, and whoever is ready to go into it will find a guide near at hand ready to lead him on. His Master awaits his bidding, and if he demand to be shown the wonders within that mystic place, they will be shown to him. This, to the seer a place, is in truth not only that, but a state or condition of the spirit in which, by its own energy and power of demand, all lessons possible to the human spirit are to be interpreted. The cathedrals, built by man on earth, are shaped according to the plan of the Hall of Learning; undoubtedly the great architects who designed them were seers, and drew their inspiration from beyond the gates of matter. When this ethereal cathedral, the one great worshiping place for all the spirits of men, is filled with worshipers, the disciple who can see perceives that the dim vault above is no roof but Heaven itself, and knows that the mysterious open space above the great altar leads to the throne of the Supreme. Chapels surround the body of the building, into which the disciples are admitted, and to which they are led by their guides. When one first is able to remain within this sacred place at the resurrection season, he finds himself taken in a strong grasp, and led across the vast floor as a little child might be led, to whatever door he has earned the right to enter. For the first time since the desire of birth brought him into matter and he became man, for the first time since he entered upon the long pilgrimage and found the path, he is utterly content knowing that he is now at home, and in his own place. The door before which he stands will be opened for him, the Master-hand will turn the handle. A great blazing diamond, flashing light to those eyes that can perceive it and can bear it, forms the handle of the door which admits to that chapel where *Light on the Path* is written on the walls, where these rules have been written from all time, where they will be written while time lasts. They vanish, if one enters who is not ready to apprehend them, and the great wall opposite the door appears to be covered with a flashing arabesque of jewels. Sometimes one who has earned the right to enter, and who is not yet able to read, will acquire that power while within the chapel; and he will then see the wonderful transition from the flame of the jewels to the flame of the words. They are written there for him, personally, as for every disciple who can read. At the Easter season a few new disciples are led within the door of this chapel every year, and a great and special effort is made by their guides and masters to enable them to read the words upon the wall.

It was inevitable and essential that, at a certain point in the history of the human race, these rules should be brought from the ethereal into the material world, written down in human language, and given to those who desired them. That I myself, who write these pages, was given the great privilege of performing this task was the result of the endurance of many bitter ordeals in successive incarnations. The experiences of human life bring the disciple continually to the places where an effort will raise him into another state. These experiences are repeated until the effort is made. A tragedy occurred in my life which I recognized, when in the midst of it, as being one I had endured many times before. This recognition enabled me to make the great effort, and climb the step indicated to me. The amazing shock and joy of the higher consciousness fell upon me; One stood beside me, in my room, and said to me, "Come, you are able to read now." I left my body, retaining a clear connection with it and

recording in my physical brain all that I did,
while I was doing it. Only by a great access
of consciousness can such a task be accomplished. The knowledge of what is being done
must be complete and full on all planes of the
being. The Master took my hand in his, and,
in full recognition of what I was doing, I held
to him, and went forth from my body, passing from matter into the ethereal space. We
entered the Hall, crossed the great floor, and
reached that door with the flashing diamond
handle—a veritable point of light. I knew
then that I had been here many times before,
and I passed the message back to my physical
brain that I was in a familiar, well-known
place, and that all was very well with me.
The Master opened the door, and entering it,
closed it behind us. We were alone in this
marvelous chapel of light. The peace and
sense of strength, the ineffable consciousness
of being in my own place, to which I had
earned the right, the inalienable right, was
an overpowering reward for the sufferings
and ordeals of earth lives. The Master, still
holding my hand, led me across the floor of

the chapel to the wall, and I saw clearly the first rules of *Light on the Path* appear at the top of it. Looking up I read them plainly; below, the jewels still flashed in glorious colorings and points of light.

"Fix these in your memory," he said to me, "take them back with you to earth, and write them down. The Teachers of the human race have decided to put these rules into human language, and you are chosen for the work. Return again and again, until you have read them all, and written them down in words upon earth."

I returned to my body, and found myself in clear possession of full memory of what I had done, and what I had seen and read. I was in the state of consciousness known to the occultists of Southern India as *jagrat of swapna*, which is the consciousness of waking clairvoyance. Only a person ignorant of occultism could suppose that it was in any way possible to bring this knowledge to earth, except by the work of a disciple who had attained to this consciousness. In no state of unconsciousness of the scribe, by no overshadowing or control of the Master, can teaching of this absolute character be obtained. I committed to memory, in that state, the first lines of the ancient, mystic writing, now known to all students of occultism under the title of *Light on the Path.* I brought it down into physical consciousness, and recorded it. I obeyed the order given to me, and, again and again, entering into the state of waking clairvoyance, returned to the chapel of light, bringing back the rules one by one, and writing them down, until I had obtained the whole.

Let none who seeks the truth lose sight of the fact that to read these words upon the wall, and to read them in the languages of earth, are two entirely different acts. Those who read them on the wall have experienced the ordeals, and attained the degree of advancement necessary for the attainment of waking clairvoyance; they read the rules with their spiritual intelligence in a state of activity, and know that the goal they indicate can only be reached after the incarnations are at an end, when the adept has passed through the higher mystic states of consciousness, and is prepared to enter into consciousness of his Logos. He can then "inquire of the inmost"; then "no law can be framed, no guide can exist."

*Light on the Path* is the trumpet-call to the spirit of man. It indicates the highest steps in the occult life, known only to the adepts. Those who read the words in human languages frequently suppose that the rules apply to human life. They are not yet ready to understand that which is beyond human life. It is for them to learn how to develop so that they shall recognize what lies beyond it. The reading of the words in human languages is useful, as it gives to the mind the idea of direction, and, if the student aims at the direction pointed out to him, more understanding arises within him. To those who are entirely enveloped in material conditions the words are meaningless.

It is a splendid thought that so many are now desirous to find the right direction that it was considered necessary to give these rules to men. The uttermost darkness is passed in

the history of the race, or this would not have
been done. The abysmal depth of blind ig-
norance and sloth does not any longer hold
the larger part of the race, or the more important part of it. Ambition, the first teacher,
has taught men something during the ages,
and in the many lives that are past. By its successive and insidious temptations, it has
drawn enough men out of the slough to form
a company which may set forth to lead the
others onward. Therefore, it is fitting that
they should know and understand in what direction they are going, and what nature it is
that they have to produce out of human
nature by the resurrection miracle, by transformation and transmutation. Therefore, are
these rules essentially the Easter lesson, to be
studied by the disciple with ceaseless vigi-
lance. Sometimes a number of disciples obtain entrance to the chapel of light at this
season, and, unable to read, kneel in devotion before the mystery of the jeweled wall,
drawing from it some of the strength left
there by the Builder, who built it before time
was, to stand firm and hold its glorious

message so long as time shall be. It is written in two parts, because it is designed as a guide to the disciple when he has secured adeptship; and when from adeptship he advances to the state of Nirvana, or absorption into the Logos, then at last the spiritual being returns into its true home. The silence which "may last a moment of time, or may last a thousand years," *but will end* is the Yoga-sleep of the adept (Rule 21). This was pointed out by T. Subba Row, the Brahman Theosophist (*Esoteric Writings*, p. 253). From this sleep, or sublime meditation, the adept is roused by a "resonant voice," which is "the silence itself." It is so, being the outcome of all human experience. The one who is "now a disciple" is commanded once more to become a student, and read what is written in the Hall of Learning for him. That which is written for him now guides him to freedom, to the place where the voice is soundless, and that which is gazed upon is invisible. This is the Nirvanic state. The story of the year, Nature and super-Nature in their action upon man, lead him in this path by continually repeated exhortation. The miracle he has to perform is shown to him yearly in the great pageant that is produced by the sun's movement northward. In the formula of the Feast of Birth, the disciple declares, "I am ready to be naked and unprotected." T. Subba Row says (*Esoteric Writings*, p. 27), in speaking of the highest stage of development known to us, "where spiritual consciousness disappears, leaving the seventh principle in a complete state of *Nirvana* or nakedness." This is the state of being at which the disciple aims, to which the path leads him; and the second part of *Light on the Path* relates solely to that high attainment.

Ambition, the first curse of the disciple, is that which raises men who live in the material conditions. To them it is the highest motive possible, and it cannot be dispensed with as a teacher of men. Let no one think he can become a disciple without the strength which can only be acquired by the strain and stress of the nature under the whip of ambition. It must be slain, it is one of the kinsmen Arjuna must kill in battle, yet it rises from its grave, and the essence of it is transformed and transmuted. For the disciple cannot enter upon the Great Task unless he knows how to work as those work who are ambitious, and he can never obtain that power to work without the training endured by the ambitious man. Ambition must have been served in its character as a hard taskmaster, and set aside as being worthless in itself, before the Master will lead his pupil from the chapel of light to the chapel of action.

# CHAPTER XI

*T*he Chapel of Action is open to all com-
ers who can enter; it is a question of
strength to obtain entrance here rather than
of devotion or spiritual intelligence. For here
the work in the world to be done by disciples
is considered and arranged by the Masters.
Those who enter find their own place, which
none else can fill, at the great table, and here
they sit and await that which shall be given
to them. Most often it is the order to undertake an apparently hopeless task which they
receive. There are two doors in this chapel,
opposite each other; during the Easter season
they stand wide open. One admits to the
Hall, and through it the great altar can be
seen, white with the tall lilies which the seer-

artists of the past have shown as growing out
of the grave itself. The other door opens on-
to a stretch of beach and that mystic water
which separates the spirit of man, while still
embodied, from the life beyond. Across this
water come those who, having left earth life
for a long period, yet have duties to perform
and to complete upon earth. They come and
sit at this table with the entities which are
the spiritual intelligences of men upon earth.
Only here, on this high plane, can man while
embodied hope to meet the friend who has
crossed the mystic waters—(those waters
which are beyond the firmament which God
called Heaven)—"spirit to spirit, ghost to
ghost." "He cannot return to me, but I can
go to him" is the plain statement of the truth.
Man can so raise his spiritual intelligence that
it may meet the pure disembodied spirit of
a lost friend, on the highest plane attainable
to man. But this can be done only by the disciple who has learned how to go forth into
the world of spirit; not even he can bring
back the spirit of one he has loved to earth
between the incarnations. Those who grieve

for loved ones taken by death, and whose eyes
are blinded by tears, cannot enter far into the
Hall of Learning, though profound devotion
and worship may enable them to enter its
doors. Just within is a chapel known as the
Chapel of Sorrow. Many enter here and go
no further. Those who no longer have any
need for this chapel never look within its
door, do not even know that the door is there.
For it is dark, and obscure, and shrouded,
so that it is easy to pass it by. Too often grief
that is truly profound enters so deeply into
the man's nature that, when he thinks he has
conquered it, he finds it again and again a
stumbling-block upon his path, even after he
has become an accepted disciple. The hunger
of his heart reawakens on this higher plane,
and he asks the Supreme why he is still separated from the one he loves. Tears of agony
and longing burst forth anew; tears of the
spirit, far more blinding than the tears of the
human being. While these tears flow he cannot see before him; and no door in the Hall
can be opened for him, even by a master-
hand, save the shrouded door of the Chapel

of Sorrow. He will be led to it and admitted, and within he will find the grave of his loved one. It is the grave of all loved ones, where all whose grief blinds them may kneel and weep. At the Easter season the door is opened readily for him to enter this secluded place within the great temple of devotion; but the secrets of that temple and its mysteries are hidden from him because of the veil of grief upon his eyes. It is not for him to reach that high place where the embodied and the disembodied may perchance meet in united action for some great cause, "spirit to spirit, ghost to ghost."

In the *Light on the Path* chapel, or chapel of light—so called because it is always illumined by the jewels on the walls, or by the greater glory of the words—there is a great Volume with clasps that can be locked. Most often the book is closed and locked. On Easter-Eve it stands open on a high reading-desk, which holds that and nothing else. It contains the pledges of disciples to undertake various tasks in the world; here come those who desire to work for humanity, and write their names in the book beneath the pledge taken by them. When this is done, they are led on to the chapel of action, where places await them at the great table, which sometimes wears the aspect of a table of work, and sometimes of a table of sacrament, with a cup of bitterness for each to drink. But in that cup is contained also the mystic transference of energy, which is the basis of the rite of the Holy Communion. If the disciple has attempted too high a step in signing his name in the book, he will faint away and vanish on the floor of the chapel, and his signature will vanish from the book. The whole effort will be wiped out as though it had not been. He may not remember it in his physical memory, but he will be haunted throughout that incarnation by a sense of an unfulfilled duty, of an unacknowledged responsibility for the world, its suffering and its sin. He cannot make this effort again in the same incarnation. If his strength endures through the taking of the mystic pledge of work, he is led on to the chapel of action, where he finds his place, and where his bitter cup awaits him.

Sooner or later it will be given him to drink.
Some faint away and vanish from their places
at this table, and are not able to return to it.
But when they have gone so far, the pledge
remains written in the book, and their names
do not vanish away but are permanent. From
time to time, when they come into the chapel
of light, the book is opened for them to look
upon their names written by their own
hands. The pledge is unfulfilled, the work remains undone. Abashed and ashamed, they
go out silently. Between the incarnations the
unfulfilled pledge holds them, and they seek
a place in the chapel of action.

On Easter Day the table in this chapel is
full; all are called to come to it who are capable of doing so. The Christ Himself sits at
the table, calling upon the Christos in the
spiritual nature of the disciples; and each
who is present drinks the wine of life.

There are many other mystic centers of
devotion and effort, surrounding the Hall as
chapels surround a cathedral, and there are
entrances and exits which are not used by
human spirits, but by the forces or powers

which are in charge of man's fate, and who affect his life according to the law of his Karma. They come here to watch the mysterious weaving of the threads of the individual Karmas of men into the great rope that is the Karma of the race. They come here to see into the hearts of those disciples who are able to enter. Death himself comes here, and bows before the altar and that open space above it. On Easter Day the spiritual shape of the last Avatar descends from this space, which opens to "the unperceived," and stands upon the altar steps to bless the crowds of worshipers. Seeing or unseeing, veiled or unveiled, all those who kneel here in true worship receive the blessing.

Between the altar and the door into the chapel of action, which is on the right hand side of it, is a small dark door which is seldom opened. Those who enter the place within are constantly there, and obtain entrance by another method. The door is fastened with an iron clamp. Another door from this place opens into the chapel of action, and on Easter Day this stands wide open, and the spiritual beings who are there pass in and out; sometimes one raises his cup to his lips, drains it to the dregs, and then rises and goes quickly through this open door right into a clear, intense flame which burns here always. Each one believes himself alone in it; each one is in fact alone in it, for no one can perceive another. This is not fire of the kind that keeps men alive; it has no material element in it; it is the bitter fire of purification, the fierce flames that rise from the crucible of life are those which consume the alloy in the trembling, quivering shapes that willingly endure the agony of standing within it. They experience pure spiritual suffering, for which there is no alleviation, which ceases not till its task is done. Therefore the disciples seek the suffering, and do not attempt to evade it, knowing that until all which is capable of being destroyed is utterly burned and consumed there is no true birthday. The spiritual part is perpetually within the flame; but with those who have not attained to the condition of waking and sleeping at the same time there are merciful intervals of unconsciousness.

The Essenes recognized as an important part of their training the cultivation of the power of retaining consciousness during the whole twenty-four hours, the spiritual intelligence keeping the physical brain informed of all that it experienced during physical sleep. The day then becomes but a brief interval spent in time and space, between timeless periods, to the disciple. But to the one who endeavors to obtain such powers without due preparation, there may be the bitter disappointment of leaving the body only to find himself imprisoned in the earth-sphere, unable even to approach the Hall of Learning; or if he can enter here, it may be but to become fully conscious of the protracted agony of purification. And then he will fall back in despair. The disciple shrinks from full consciousness until he is fully prepared, because it may mean constant suffering. So the ordinary man fears Death, having an inner knowledge that he will have to endure many things at the hands of that great king. It is not right to despise men who fear death; they are those who have yet to climb many difficult steps before they can pass the portals of the body in confidence and hope. No step in the great Path can be taken hastily without regret, and too often haste necessitates the retracing of the step. "Grow as the flower grows," eager, yet absolutely obedient to the laws which govern it, so that its unfoldment is gradual yet perfect. The *jagrat of swapna,* or waking clairvoyance, is that state in which *Light on the Path* can be read on the wall where it is written.

*MAY*
*Transmutation*

# CHAPTER XII

*T*hat miracle which the disciple has to accomplish consists of what must be regarded as two acts, transformation and transmutation. The first may be defined as the changing of the heart of the man. While he is transforming himself, he is the Arjuna of the *Bhagavad Gita*. The climax of this effort is reached on an Easter Day when he consciously enters the Chapel of Fire and remains willingly within the flame. Hitherto he has been fighting upon the battlefield of his nature, conquering evil desires and destroying evil passions. That the foes he has to fight cannot actually be killed is laid down very plainly in the speech of the Deity in Chapter XI of the *Bhagavad Gita*, when He explains to Arjuna that he has already slain them, yet says, "Do fight;—Whom I have killed, do you kill."[1] This attitude of fighting, of killing out ambition, desire of life, desire of comfort, the sense of separateness, the desire for sensation, the hunger for growth, is that which effects the transformation of the man's own heart. But it has to be followed by the second part of the miracle, transmutation, the divine alchemy. This process is indicated in *Light on the Path* in the rules, "Work as those work who are ambitious. Respect life as those do who desire it. Be happy as those are who live for happiness." Not only has the heart of man to be transformed so that he kills out ambition, and the thirst for life and comfort, but he must utilize the forces in his nature which cause these passions, and transmute them so that he can use them for the great end and object of being, for the service of the Supreme. It is for this that he endures the burning in the crucible of life. This is the application to his own

---

[1]P. 96, Max Müller's translation

nature of that alchemy which he is bidden to use towards super-Nature, and the great forces which act upon and through it, in the formula of the Ceremony of the Feast of Love.

The curtains which fall between the consciousnesses, veiling them from one another completely, have to be lifted so that there is always a passage through from one to the other. Only for the adept can the veil be entirely lifted. The disciple has to be content with a narrow way through which he can just pass, with a sufficient space to look through always kept open, and this is only possible by the help of a Master—help such as that which is given to enable a disciple to read *Light on the Path*. It consists in showing the disciple how to sustain the condition of waking clairvoyance. If he is able to sustain that, he can pass on alone. Such help is most readily found at the Easter season, which is followed by the wondrous month of transmutation, during which the lifting of the veil into another consciousness should be effected, and can be effected by one who has passed successfully through the preparatory ordeals. At the Easter season we celebrate the great fundamental religious idea of arising from the grave, of the Spirit of Man, the Christos, emerging from the tomb of the place of darkness in the animal soul. This celebration, now universally known as Eastertide, comes, by the force of supernatural workings, in the spring; the word simply means springtide. The arising from winter gloom is past; the green leaves are now opening. The disciple must enter with resolution upon the task of personal development during the period of full foliage and the flowering of Nature. The harvest will soon come, that yearly reckoning; the tree will be known by its fruit. It is now that the disciple must fully test his own nature, and cling to the highest standard of conduct that he can perceive, hoping to reach a yet higher standard when the birth month is again reached in the yearly drama.

The Yoga prescribed in *Light on the Path* existed before the founding of Buddhism, before Gautama Buddha was born. The idea expressed in the word *Yoga* is that of union with the Supreme. The derivation is from the Sanskrit root, "yuj," to join; we have in the English word yoke a similar conception. The disciple desires to become yoked with the One who rules all, and eventually to enter so completely into the action of the divine good as to become one with it, united with it. To attain this end has the Indian Yogi suffered the extremes of physical martyrdom; to attain this end did Guatama Buddha go to the Brahman ascetics and learn from them the practice of Yoga.

The first four of the five evil acts to be avoided on entering upon the practice of Yoga correspond to the first four commandments of Buddhism; the first one in each is "Kill not." As Sir Edwin Arnold expresses it, "Kill not—lest ye slay the meanest thing upon its upward way." Life is the gift of the Supreme to all creatures, by which they may suffer and obtain purification, and seek union with the life-giver. The first injunction in the Patanjali Yoga, the first commandment in Buddhism, stands as the fourth rule in the stanzas of *Light on the Path*. This is because, with the development of the human race, ambition, love of personal life, and personal comfort have taken so strong a hold upon the nature of man that they must be encountered and destroyed before the practice of Yoga can commence. To the ancient Brahman Yogi such desires would have been puerile, beneath contempt, unthinkable. The Western world is more deeply plunged in the slough of materialism; ambition has been necessary to draw it forth from the abyss. When ambition is destroyed, the objects of ambition must be destroyed with it; the love of personal life and personal comfort are the motives of the ambitious man. And now comes, in *Light on the Path*, that further exposition of "Respect life as those do who desire it." This is the first part of the divine alchemy, the transmutation of his lower self into the higher being which shall be worthy of immortality, upon which the disciple enters so soon as his Spiritual intelligence emerges from the Tomb. He has no longer any desire of life; the desire of birth has exhausted itself. But he sees that in asking for life and obtaining it, he made the great step towards union with the Supreme, and received the great boon which shall enable him to reach his goal. Therefore he respects his own life as though he desired it; therefore he respects the life of all other beings equally. The mere possession of this gift, which can only be obtained from the Supreme, is sufficient to show that the creature possessing it has the great opportunity of passing on the upward way.

The disciple, in entering upon this transmutation, must recognize his duty towards the outer world, of which he is an inalienable part, at every step. The greater number of the followers of the Buddha and the Christ have refused to avoid this evil action of killing, and have, therefore, been unable to enter upon the practice of Yoga. The meat-eating Tibetan Buddhists are said to have employed Chinese Mohammedans to slay animals (in a most cruel manner), thus hoping to evade the bad Karma of the evil deed. But this evasion is not possible. He who eats the meat is the one for whom the butchery is committed, and is therefore the chief culprit and breaker of the divine law. This attempt to avoid the burden of the sin is not adopted in the West; it would be absurd in countries where sport is glorified and regarded as a royal and noble pastime. Those who are attempting the path of Yoga in the midst of modern civilization undertake a very severe task. The very first step is one which places them altogether apart from ordinary men. And those who have attained the power of waking clairvoyance, and have read *Light on the Path* upon the walls of the chapel of light, know that no negative state of personal non-killing is sufficient. In the midst of cities full of butchery, of countrysides made hideous by it, of nations possessed by the passion of sport and devoted to the cult of war, he has to *"respect life."* And that force within him which enabled him to be born, which was desire of life, has, with his change of heart, to be destroyed in its first shape, seized and transmuted into the divine "respect for life." His task is no easy one, and will pursue him, partially fulfilled, from year to year, from life to life.

Now, with the green leaves of Nature, the bursting forth of the earth's life, comes the time when the disciple must see to it that the green leaves of his own higher nature unfold truly. When he enters into the state of waking clairvoyance, many things will become plain to him which have hitherto been inexplicable, and he will perceive the inner working of the life of the world. He will realize that he cannot enter upon the path of Yoga until he has not only avoided the evil deeds which are forbidden, but has faced that evil force which causes them, and compelled it, in his immediate neighborhood, to change its very nature and to share in the transmutation which he is himself undergoing. He cannot be separated from that in which he exists; he must purify the air he breathes and all with which he comes into contact, as he himself is purified. Thus is the world to be redeemed. In the course of this supreme effort, the risen spirit lifts all that surrounds it, by spiritual power, so that the very ground on which the man treads has new life within it where his footsteps pass.

Take emotion and make it purpose, says the Master. The heart has to be watched and searched ceaselessly, in order to make of its passions and storms not sensations which sweep the man hither and thither, but weapons of actions to be used in the great crusade of the infinite against the finite, the spiritual against the material. And the risen spirit knows that these weapons are not weapons of offense, which have long been forsworn and laid aside, for finite is but an aspect of the infinite, the material of the spiritual. The weapons are indeed no longer such as Arjuna even would use against the kinsmen who are already slain by the Deity, but have become rather tools than weapons, tools with which to remodel the aspect of the human being. The heart of the disciple has, during the past vigils, been purged of its lower passions; now, when assailed by the pairs of opposites, it may no longer suffer and be silent or take enjoyment with thankfulness; it is the heart of a risen spirit with power to move in the

ethereal spaces, with power to read the hearts
of others. It must create out of those emotions
which still assail it, a vital, moving purpose.
To the man who is becoming a disciple, and
compelling his own nature to obey dictates
from above, life is like a long fever, full of
struggle, illuminated by visions, sometimes
darkened by delirium. Now that the miracle
of Easter has been accomplished in the
history of the individual being in its earthly
pilgrimage, the Master bids the disciple not
to quell this fever, but to transform it into
force. Thus the leaders and reformers on the
material plane arise, filled with the passion
for good, hungry for the effort of all towards
progress. No longer may the one who seeks
the way retire into obscurity and dwell like
a hermit. The trumpet-call has been
sounded. The world must be aroused, enlightened, stirred to its depths. The menace
of madness stands ever before the one who
makes the great effort in the midst of the ser-
ried ranks of the enemy, the hostile kinsmen.
This is no real menace, for the disciple who
has reached the stage of transmutation has
power to change the quivering of the spirit,

and the turmoil of the brain, into the perfect
calm of divine confidence. He has only to
look towards the Supreme, which is his Guide
and his Goal.

In the Buddhist religion the month of May
is recognized as the time for the risen spirit
to manifest its power and character. On the
first, the birth of the Buddha is celebrated;
on the fifth, the revelation of the esoteric doctrine by the Buddha to his disciples is com-
memorated. In the Brahmanical system this
is a month for sacrificial sessions. The sanctity of the springtide is truly traced to a solar
origin, and the vivifying power of the life
now poured upon the earth is recognized and
used to the uttermost in spiritual experience.

The transmutation of feeling into power,
of life into thought, of madness into divine
confidence, have nothing to do with the
struggle between good and evil, for the disciple has passed through purification. It has to
do with another pair of opposites, which now
arise like an insurmountable barrier in the
path. But when approached with divine confidence by a risen spirit possessed of the gift
of waking clairvoyance, there is a way to be

perceived. It is that of the conversion of what is negative in the nature to that which is positive. The whole entity must proclaim itself an emissary of the Most High, a light-bringer.

It is related of the Bodhisattva that once, at the close of an incarnation, at the moment of death, expiring in his forest-home, he exclaimed: "Neither conscious nor unconscious!" The recluses did not believe the interpretation given to these words by the chief disciple. The Bodhisattva therefore returned from the Radiant Realm, and from mid-air recited this stanza, which concerns the transmutation of the nature of man when encountering the last pair of opposites on his path:

"*With conscious, with unconscious, too,*
*Dwells sorrow. Either ill eschew.*
*Pure bliss, from all corruption free,*
*Springs but from Insight's ecstasy.*"[2]

Ecstasy is the state to be attained by the risen spirit, one of the early states of con-

---

[2]From *The Jataka*

sciousness open to the adepts. Beyond it lie mystic conditions which cannot be described in printed words.

As each initiation is passed, a curtain is drawn aside for the spiritual intelligence of the disciple to hold back, or to let fall at his own will. Now, in the time of the full spring-tide, the consummation of the resurrection, the spirit holds these curtains in his hands, and looks back down the vista to his first step on the path. He can enter now into the higher mystic consciousness if he has no step to retrace, no fault to amend, no debt to pay.

In Tibet the anniversary of Buddha's Nirvana is kept near the first of June. This closes the six sacred months. The task of the risen spirit is now to press steadily onwards and upwards to a higher birth in the coming birth month. The inconceivable increase of individual consciousness to be attained by becoming united with the Logos may be dimly perceived on reflecting that this union opens the way into the consciousness of the other Logoi.